Moses Margoliouth

Vestiges of the Historic Anglo-Hebrews in East Anglia

With appendices and an apropos essay

Moses Margoliouth

Vestiges of the Historic Anglo-Hebrews in East Anglia
With appendices and an apropos essay

ISBN/EAN: 9783337418403

Printed in Europe, USA, Canada, Australia, Japan

Cover: Foto ©ninafisch / pixelio.de

More available books at **www.hansebooks.com**

VESTIGES

OF THE

HISTORIC ANGLO-HEBREWS

IN

EAST ANGLIA.

WITH APPENDICES AND AN APROPOS ESSAY.

BY

THE REV. M. MARGOLIOUTH, LL.D., PH.D.,
ETC., ETC.

AUTHOR OF "A PILGRIMAGE TO THE LAND OF MY FATHERS," "THE HISTORY
OF THE JEWS IN GREAT BRITAIN," ETC., ETC.

LONDON:
LONGMANS, GREEN, READER, AND DYER.

1870.

TO

SIR ROBERT PIGOT, BART.,

THIS VOLUME IS,

WITH SENTIMENTS OF GREAT REGARD AND SINCERE ESTEEM,

RESPECTFULLY INSCRIBED

BY

THE AUTHOR.

PREFACE.

THIS volume is one of the effects issuing from the labours of the "Royal Archæological Institute for Great Britain and Ireland." Having been asked, in the spring of this year, by some friends interested in the researches and prosperity of that useful Association, to contribute a paper at their annual meeting, to be held this year at Bury St. Edmund's; I acquiesced, and fixed upon the subject which gives the title to this publication. I considered it a proper theme for an Essay to be brought under the notice of an assembly of archæologists, who were to meet in the town which bears the name of one of the kings of the East Angles. The subject commended itself to the Honorary Secretary of the Institute, and I forthwith set to work to isolate some materials for this particular purpose, from MSS. on kindred subjects, upon which many a year's hard work and study had been bestowed.

When I had arranged the joints of my skeleton, I began to feel apprehensive about its probable proportions, should I venture to clothe it with the sinews, flesh, and skin commensurate with its gigantic stature. I therefore, by sundry expedients, reduced the structure of my skeleton to a dwarfish size; but even then I was dubious as to whether it might not be considered out of proportion, for the time usually allowed for one paper. It took me nearly three hours to accomplish a private perusal of the first abridgment. The dissecting knife was once more applied, and a further series of excisions achieved. Naturally, I had my misgivings as to the effect which the mutilated and maimed thesis might produce upon a highly educated audience, such as form the attendance at such conferences. I confess that whilst I hoped for the best, I was prepared for the worst. However, the meeting was kinder to me than my apprehensions foreboded.

It was my good fortune to read my paper when a NOBLEMAN, well worthy of the name, an accomplished Scholar, and a learned Divine—then the Venerable Lord Arthur Hervey, Archdeacon of Sudbury, now Bishop of Bath and Wells—occupied the chair. The President's generous indulgence seemed to permeate and pervade the whole audience. I had an attentive and encouraging hearing—notwithstanding the great length of my paper, mutilated though it was—accorded to me. That was not all. When I had finished, the noble President, as well as the assembly generally, was good enough to speak in terms of commendation of my humble performance. I was asked by many, then and there, to publish the production; and often, since then, have I been importuned to give the "*opuscula, pro bono publico*." Refusing compliance might have been construed into an affected modesty. I have deferred therefore to the wishes of my partial critics, as I must call those friends who have urged on the publication of this paper. In doing so, I have restored, in the shape of notes and appendices, some of the parings which I had made from the original plan; and have also added an apropos Essay, on the qualifications which the historian of Jewish annals must possess.

It is not improbable that some of the readers of this Brochure, may be already acquainted with my works on the annals of the Anglo-Hebrews,—namely, "The Jews in Great Britain; being a Series of Six Lectures delivered at the Liverpool Collegiate Institution, on the Antiquities of the Jews in England," and "The History of the Jews in Great Britain"—such would no doubt feel somewhat struck at my altered interpretation of certain men and things, words, thoughts, and deeds, from that propounded in my former works. "Live and learn," though a trite saying, is yet a true and sound aphorism. The first-named work was written upwards of a quarter century ago; the second more than a score of years ago. One learns, and has to unlearn, a great deal during such a period of time. On several subjects, I frankly own, my opinions were then formed on imperfect information, and but crudely digested. Twenty years' hard reading, travelling, and thinking, wonderfully enlarge one's information, and ripen considerably one's judgment.

Let me instance two of the principal features in the following pages—the purport of the bronze vessel found in a Suffolk river, (p. 46,) and the identification of Nicolaus de Lyra with a Franciscan Monk of Lynn, (p. 56.) When I first treated of the former, I was led principally by Dr. Tovey's account of the vessel. I then lived far away from Town, and could not avail myself of the unpublished literary treasures of the British Museum. The sketch of the vessel—the *fac simile* of which forms the *frontispiece*—as preserved amongst the MSS. of the National Archives, is as different as possible from the print of the same vessel, as given by Dr. Tovey.* I had not then visited Prague, and had not read the "Sermons in Stone," with which the ancient Jewish cemetery, in that place, abounds. When I first treated of Nicolaus de Lyra, I was not aware that there flourished a Nicolaus de Lynn at the latter part of the thirteenth, and the early part of the fourteenth, century. My former works, just named, are out of print; I am prepared for a new History of the Jews in Great Britain, up to the present day, founded on materials carefully collected, and critically sifted, since the publication of the works alluded to.

Let me close my few prefatory remarks with a hope that my readers will accord to me the like indulgence which my hearers have done; and will generously credit me with a conscientious desire to give them the truest attainable information in my power, weeded of the tares which ignorance, prejudice, bigotry, and superstition disseminate.

M. M.

Branches Park, Newmarket,
  December 1869.

* The stamp on the cover is a miniature of Lady Pigot's grand artistic diagram, which her Ladyship kindly prepared, for the purpose of illustrating the part of the paper which it concerned. (P. 46.)

THE VESTIGES

OF THE

HISTORIC ANGLO-HEBREWS OF EAST ANGLIA.

WITTINGLY, or unwittingly, the Royal Archæological Institute, in common with certain other scientific and literary unions, has an important mission. The congress, moving about from place to place in the United Kingdom, affords an opportunity to Englishmen everywhere to learn from the past how to improve the present, and how to provide against the future.

There are cycles in history as well as in nature; both are ordained and controlled by the first great cause, the moral governor of the universe; both are intended to inculcate the sublimest of lessons. They point thoughtful minds retrospectively and prospectively. When our physical eyes are strained by gazing at eclipses, conjunctions of planets, the reappearance of certain comets, meteoric showers, &c., our mental eyes look back upon the world and the inhabitants thereof, when the same phenomena took place in times past. We have before our mind's eye the men and women who walked this earth then, who hoped and feared, loved and hated, did good and evil; some were meek, and some were arrogant; some were gentle, and some were rude and rough. They gazed then on the same objects as we now gaze. Where are they?

Our eye of imagination pierces through also the vista of futurity. We contemplate beings beholding the same wondrous things in years to come; when we shall be gathered hence. Verily, the revolving cycles of nature are great moralists and levellers.

The same feelings and thoughts impress us when we roam over the sites of ancient cities and temples; such as Thebes, Memphis, Heliopolis, Nimroud, Ninevah, Baalbeck, Palmyra, Ephesus, Corinth, Carthage, Sidon, Tyre, Jerusalem; or to begin at home— the ancient Castles, Cathedrals, Minsters, Abbeys, Monasteries and Convents of Old England. The same eclipses, the same conjunctions of planets, the same comets, the same meteoric showers interested the teeming multitudes who once lived, moved, and had their beings in all those places. Where are they now?

The periodical bringing before the world the vestiges and traces of our predecessors, is intended, like the revolving cycles of nature, to enforce the truth taught by the inspired penman: "O my God, Thy years are throughout all generations. Of old hast Thou laid the foundation of the earth; and the heavens are the work of Thy hands. They shall perish; but Thou shalt endure, yea all of them shall wax old like a garment; as a vesture shalt Thou change them, and they shall be changed: but Thou art the same, and Thy years shall have no end. The children of Thy servants shall continue, and their seed shall be established before Thee."*

Such thoughts are induced by the researches of archæological, literary, and scientific institutions. The researches of those organisations spread a table at which the minds of all sorts of literati can feast; at which the wisdom of the profoundest savants may grow stronger and stronger; and the crumbs which fall from it must be nourishing to the masses. The respective Councils make good use of their opportunities; they hold their meetings annually in different parts of the kingdom, so that they make their existence to be felt all over this realm, and thus awaken inquiry, and set intelligent minds to think of the things that have been, that are, and that may be.

There is one branch of archæological and historical research which may be compared to a tree which has taken deep root in every part of the earth, whose shadow covers every hill, and whose boughs are like mighty cedars. The fruit thereof may serve as the most nourishing aliment for the mind of every nation under heaven. Or, to use a metaphor befitting the present occasion, it is that of a shattered ruin of the most magnificent temple which the Great Architect of the universe had ever designed, and which the Grand Master Mason had ever reared, whose fragments have been scattered over "the wide, wide world." It is the archæology and history of the Jewish people. The interest which that history awakens is cosmopolitan in character, inasmuch as the outcasts of Judah,

* Psalm cii. 24—28.

and the dispersed of Israel, are everywhere to be found. Go from Moscow to Lisbon, from Borneo to Archangel, from Hindustan to Honduras, from Japan to Britain, and you will meet in the course of your multifarious peregrinations, with representatives of the scattered but sacred race. He that adventures himself to the snows of Siberia, meets with Jews there; he who traverses the sands of the burning desert, encounters members of the tribes of that wandering race; the European traveller hears of their existence in regions which he cannot reach. Surely, there must be a great and instructive design in the dispersion of that ancient people, for the improvement of mankind all over the world.

Of late years, this branch of archæology has enlisted the interest of the devout, learned, and curious; and in no country more so than in this. I venture to hope that this paper may conduce to the stirring up of critical enquiry and research into the early annals of the Jews in this country. I am only dealing this time with a few fragments of the great theme, even *the Vestiges of the Historic Anglo-Hebrews of East Anglia.*

As this subject, in an exclusive paper, is for the first time treated in the annals of the Royal Archæological Institute, I may perhaps be pardoned if I advert, for a few moments, to the earliest acquaintance of some of the sacred race with this island. I do not apprehend any successful contradiction when I state that some Jews may have dated their earliest landing on British soil, long ere Romans, Saxons, Danes, or Normans coveted the possession of the British isle. I have elsewhere demonstrated* the migratory character of the Hebrew race, and the reason thereof, ever since "the Father of the faithful," *i.e.*, their Patriarch Abraham, was enjoined to get him out of his country, and from his kindred, and from his father's house, unto a land that would be shown him; and promised that he should be made a great nation.† I have already established a strong probability that some Jews were personally acquainted with this "isle afar off" from their own land, as early as the time of Solomon, when that monarch's navy accompanied that of Tyre and Sidon.‡ That opinion, which I formed on the strength of irrefragable evidence, I still maintain, the ingenious arguments of the late Sir George C. Lewis notwithstanding. Sir Edward S. Creasy, in his "History of England from the Earliest Times," the first volume of which has just been published, after careful research and critical examination of evidence, has come to the mature conviction that "the British tin mines mainly supplied the glorious adornment of Solomon's Temple."

A small remnant of that monarch's subjects remained in Cornwall since that time I have traced that remnant by the paths of philology, and the byways of nomenclature. I might adduce an array of whole sentences, exactly alike in the languages of Hebrew and the ancient Cornish.§ I might adduce some of the proper names which prevailed amongst the aboriginal Britons long before they knew any-

* "The Jews in Great Britain."   † Genesis xii. 1, 2.
‡ "The Jews in Great Britain."   § See Appendix A.

thing of Christianity, such as Adam, Abraham, Asaph, Benyon, Daniel, Solomon, of which latter name the ancient Britons, according to Lloyd's Cambria, had three kings. We read of a Duke of Cornwall, Solomon by name, openly professing Christianity about the middle of the fourth century. Solomon was not his baptismal name, but one by which he was known before that sacrament was administered to him.

Let me just glance at a few fragments, from the ruins of Jewish history, to show that considerable numbers of the sacred, scattered nation were in this island in the time of the Romans. A copy of a letter preserved by the Jewish apocryphal historian, Josephon ben Gorion, which the Jews of Asia sent to Hyrcanus and the nobles of Judah, contains the following passage:—" Be it know unto you, that Augustus Cæsar, by the advice of his ally, Antoninus, has sent throughout all the countries of his dominions, as far as beyond the Indian sea, and as far as beyond the land of Britain, that is, the land in the midst of the ocean, and commanded that in whatever place there be man or woman of the Jewish race, man servant, or maid servant, to set them free without any redemption money. By command of Cæsar Augustus and his ally Antoninus." *

In the *Tzemach David*, a Hebrew Chronicle of some importance, written by Rabbi David Ganz, we have the following brief record : " Cæsar Augustus was a pious and God-fearing man, and did execute judgment and justice, and was a lover of Israel.

* See Appendix B.

And as to that which is reported at the commencement of the book, 'Sceptre of Judah,' that Cæsar Augustus caused a great slaughter amongst the Jews, the informant misled the author; for I have not met with a hint even, respecting it, in all the chronicles that I have ever seen. On the contrary, in all their [*i.e.*, Gentiles'] annals, and also in the fifteenth chapter of Josephon, it is recorded that he was a faithful friend of Israel. The same writer records, in the forty-seventh chapter, that this Cæsar sent an epistle of release to the Jews in all the countries of his dominion; to the east as far as beyond the Indian sea, and to the west as far as beyond the British territory (which is the country Angleterre, and which is designated England in the vernacular.)" * The Jews in this country chronicle the same event annually, in their calendar, in the following words: "C. Æ. 15. Augustus' edict in favour of the Jews in England."

The enquiring archæologist into the antiquities of the Jews in this country, encounters the same difficulty which the wise Gildas experienced. That proto-Anglo-historian lamented in the beginning of his epistle, in which he has undertaken to give some account of the ancient British Church, the want of any domestic monuments to afford him certain information. "For," saith he, "if there were any such, they were either burnt by our enemies, or carried so far by the banishment of our countrymen, that they no

* See Appendix C.

longer appear; and therefore I was forced to pick up what I could out of foreign writers, without any continued series." So it is with the archæologist who desires to construct a history of the Anglo-Hebrews previous to their banishment from this country in 1290. We have, nevertheless, proof positive that the Jews were settled in this country to a significant extent, as has been already stated, before either Roman, Saxon, Dane, or Norman found their way hither.

Gildas' performance is not redolent of interest of any kind, and affords evidence neither one way or the other. The very next English author, the Venerable Bede, incidentally mentions the Jews, in such a manner as to prove that they must have been in this country anterior to his time. Bede, in describing some of the controversies which raged between the Romish and the British Monks, mentions the festival of Easter as a *casus belli*. The Britons celebrated Easter on the very day of the full moon in March, if that day fell on Sunday, instead of waiting till the Sunday following. The Britons pleaded the antiquity of their usage; the Romans insisted on the universality of theirs. In order to render the former odious, the latter affirmed that the native priests once in seven years concurred with the Jews in the time of celebrating that festival.

This incidental circumstance proves that there must have been Jews in Britain, where they had synagogues, and observed the feast of Passover. The Jews must also have had learned men amongst them to arrange their calendars: and such an arrangement requires a fair astronomical knowledge, or else the charge would have been totally unintelligible to the Saxons. This charge, moreover, accounts for the edict published soon after by Ecgbright, Archbishop of York, in the " Canonical Excerptiones," A.D. 740, to the effect that no Christian should be present at any of the Jewish feasts.* That edict establishes the facts that the Jews must have resided in this country at the time of the heptarchy in considerable numbers, and celebrated their feasts according to their own law; and what is more, that they desired to live peaceably with their Christian neighbours.

It also appears from a charter, granted by Whitglaff, King of the Mercians, to Croyland Abbey, ninety-three years after the above edict was issued, that there were Jews in this country at that period, and that they possessed landed property to some extent; and, what is more remarkable still, they endowed Christian places of worship. Ingulphus, in his " History of Croyland Abbey," relates that in the

* The 146th paragraph of the " Canonical Excerptiones" of Archbishop Ecgbright runs thus : " *A Laodicean Act.*—That no Christian presume to judaize, or be present at Jewish feasts." To which Johnson, in his collection of *Ecclesiastical Laws and Canons*, adds, " By this, one would suppose there were in this age Jews in the north of England. The following is the 149th paragraph of the same " Canonical Excerptiones " : "*A Canon of the Saints.*—If any Christian sell a Christian into the hands of Jews or Gentiles, let him be anathema: for it is written in Deuteronomy, 'If any man be caught trafficking for any of the stock of Israel, and take a price for him, he shall die."—*Johnson's Collection of Ecclesiastical Laws.*

year 833, Whitglaff, King of the Mercians, having been defeated by Egbert, took refuge in that Abbey, and in return for the protection and assistance rendered him by the Abbot and Monks on the occasion, granted a charter, confirming to the Abbey all lands, tenements, and possessions, and all other gifts which had at any time been bestowed upon them by his predecessors, or by any other faithful Christians, or by Jews.*

Lindo, in his very learned "Jewish Calendar for sixty-four years," published in 1838, chronicles the following:—" C. Æ. 1020. Canute banished the Jews from England." Basnage also asserts that the Jews were banished from this country in the beginning of the eleventh century, and did not return till after the Norman conquest. The authority upon which these two statements rest is not given. On the contrary, there is cogent evidence that Jews resided in England towards the middle of the eleventh century, and prior to the invasion of William I. By the laws attributed to Edward the Confessor, it is declared "that the Jews, wheresoever they be, are under the King's guard and protection; neither can any one of them put himself under the protection of any rich man without the King's license, for the Jews and all they have belong to the King; and if any person shall detain them or their

* "Omnes terras, et tenementas, possessiones, et eorum peculia, quæ roges Merciorum, et eorum Proceres, vel alii fideles Christiani, vel Judæi dictis Monarchis dederunt."

money, the King may claim them, if he pleases, as his own."*

So much for the pre-Norman Conquest Jews of this country. The few rays of historic evidence which pierce through that dark unhistoric period, converge to point out that a few of the dispersed of Judah had found their way into this country as early as the Phœnicians; that a good sprinkling of that race settled here during the Roman occupation, when they chose the principal garrisoned places of the island for their local habitation, and their early synagogues; such as London, Lincoln, York, Norwich, Leicester. Those places were selected, after the withdrawal of the Roman legions, for monastic establishments, to which were added such institutions as Oxford, Cambridge, Bury St. Edmund's, &c., &c. As all the intelligence and learning, such as they were, among the mongrel and mixed Gentile races, were then confined to those ecclesiastical and scholastical organizations, some of the Jews remained in their orginal settlements, and others repaired to the newly established places of learning and religion. In those places they lived on friendly terms with their Christian neighbours; the former making grants even of land and other property, to the abbeys and monasteries of the latter. They

* 22. *De Judæis.*—" Sciendum quoque quod omnes Judæi ubicunque in regno sunt sub tutela et defensione Regis ligea debent esse, nec quilebet eorum alicui diviti se potest subdere sine Regis licentia. Judæi enim et omnia sua Regis sunt. Quod si quispiam detinuerit eos vel pecuniam eorum, perquirat Rex si vult tanquam suum proprium."—*Spelman's Concilia Decreta, &c., vol. i., p.* 623.

felt no compunction in holding social intercourse at their fêtes and festivals, when not interfered with by fanatical or over zealous hierarchs. The Jews had already well organised schools in London, York, Oxford, Lincoln, Cambridge, Norwich, Lynn, Bury St. Edmund's, and other towns. Those schools were attended by the higher classes of Christians as well as by the Anglo-Hebrews. Some of those seminaries were more colleges than mere schools. Besides the Hebrew and Arabic languages, which were thoroughly taught in those schools, a sound education was also given in Geometry, Algebra, Astronomy, Logic, Music, Chemistry, Medicine, in those Jewish scholastic establishments; and the head masters were generally distinguished rabbis. Not the slightest hint occurs anywhere of any misdemeanor, or misconduct, on the part of the Anglo-Hebrews, previous to the Norman conquest, nor during the reign of the first three Norman Kings in this country.

Soon after the Norman conqueror had established his rule in this land, the British synagogues received a large accession of Continental Jews, and those of East Anglia among the rest. During the Conqueror's lifetime, there is every reason to believe the Jews were permitted to enjoy the sunshine of prosperity, to thrive in their various avocations peaceably and quietly. The King took them under his special care,* but did nothing which would gender jealousies and hostilities between his subjects who professed to

* The wording of the charter is pretty much the same as that of Edward the Confessor. See note on preceding page.

follow the law, and those who professed to have been converted to the Gospel.

William Rufus seemed disposed to patronise his Hebrew subjects even more than his sire did; but his patronage proved the germ of a prolific harvest of misery and wretchedness to the *proteges*. Being of an irreligious turn of mind, William II. moreover betrayed a bias for making sport of religion by setting his Jewish and Christian subjects to play at theological polemics. He thus aroused the most passionate animosities of the combatants towards each other. Not long after his accession to the throne of England, he surprised the Church and the Synagogue by summoning to the metropolis the Bishops of the former, and the Rabbis of the latter, for the express purpose of discussing the evidences and merits of their respective creeds. He took his favourite oath—by St. Luke's face—that if the Jews got the better in the dispute, he would embrace Judaism himself. At the conclusion—as is generally the case in public theological controversies—both parties claimed the victory. The effect of the dispute was that the heads of the Church had conceived a Hamanic antipathy towards the Jews, and the chiefs of the Synagogue began to deport themselves with a Mordecai-scorn towards their Christian neighbours. The bitter feeling became aggravated by the Jews having induced the King, by bribes, to force such of their nation as became Israelites indeed, that is, such as professed the whole of the Jewish religion;—not only that part which was veiled in allegory and illustrated by symbol, in the Old Testament, but also that part which unveiled and revealed the brightness of its glory in the person of Him who declared "It is finished."—"Jewish Converts," the Gentiles style such Israelites, " forgetting in the confusion of ideas," as the author of "A Political Biography" observes, that the Gentiles are the converts, and not the Jews; the latter are but "the natural branches graffed into their own olive tree." Bear with the digression.*

Well, then, to return to the thread of my narrative. The nominal Jews bribed the king to compel the "Israelites indeed" to renounce the creed which conviction and conscience prompted them to confess; for there were then many eminent Jews in this country, and especially in East Anglia, who became zealous advocates of the doctrine taught in the New Testament. William was not above becoming the required tool to bring about the desired apostacy.† That

* This looseness of talk, "this confusion of ideas," is owing its existence to the great ignorance which prevails respecting the grandest chapter in the history of the world—even that relating to the ushering in of the Christian dispensation. That wonderful chapter tells us that Jewish believers in Christ were first called Christians, (Acts xi. 26,) and not Gentile converts to the Christian religion. The latter eventually monopolised the name as well as the promises made to the "Israel of God." (Gal. vi. 16.) The Apostle evidently means, by "Israel of God," Jewish followers of Christ Jesus. As for residuary Israel—those who oppose themselves to the "New Covenant" dispensation— "He that is holy, He that is true, He that hath the key of David, He that openeth and no man shutteth, and shutteth and no man openeth," emphatically and positively denieth them the appellation "Jews." (Rev. ii. 9; iii. 9.)

† See Appendix D.

prince, of unenviable notoriety, added insult to the injury which he had already inflicted upon the Church, and thus heaped fuel upon the unholy fire of animosity which he had already kindled. When a see, abbacy, or benefice fell vacant, of which he happened to be the patron, he was in the habit of retaining it in his own hands until he became acquainted with its revenues, and then selling it to the highest bidder. The royal simonist used, whenever the opportunity occurred, to appoint Jews to take care of the vacant benefices, to farm them, and to manage the negociations for his benefit. Thus he dealt for five years with the revenues of the see of Canterbury, after Lanfranc's death; and thus he treated for three years the abbacy of Bury St. Edmund's, after the death of Baldwin. As far as the historic Anglo-Hebrews were concerned, William Rufus' reign was most advantageous to their prosperity, in a worldly point of view.

Equally so was the long reign of Henry I. The Jews are mentioned but seldom in the annals of his government, the omission may be considered as a sure token that no evil had befallen them. They strengthened their positions in their places of residence in East Anglia, built synagogues—of which Moyses' Hall, at Bury St. Edmund's, is a fair specimen—zealously preached their version of Judaism, and actually attempted to proselytise amongst the Gentile converts to Christianity. The learning and the influence of the Jewish sages of Norfolk, of this time, are frequently quoted in the Hebrew literature of the middle ages. The Church found it necessary to send the most accomplished monks to several towns in which the Jews were numerously established, for the express purpose of preaching down Judaism. In East Anglia, Cambridge and Cottenham are particularly mentioned as some of the places to which monks, from Croyland Abbey, were sent to preach against the Jews. The latter may have had their zeal provoked by some benefactions to the Church, on the part of " Israelites indeed," in different parts of the kingdom. In that of East Anglia I may mention Manasses—whose name at once reveals his nationality—a powerful Norman Baron, founded a convent for nuns at Redlingfield. About the same time the old monastery founded by Fursæus, a holy Scot, at Burgh Castle, near Yarmouth, into which King Sigibert is said to have retired after his conversion, became the property and residence of a Jewish family. None but a family of Israelites indeed would then have made their abode in that of a Christian order. The ruins of that monastery were to be seen about 150 years ago; there was then an old road leading to the principal entrance, which went by the name of " the Jews' Way."*

* A friend of mine, the Rev. J. J. Raven, of Yarmouth, who has lately visited Burgh Castle, in the course of a letter thus adverts to the above monastery :—" The remains of the Priory now form part of the Rectory out-buildings. There is very little left—the base of a short flint wall, of which the upper part is later, containing, however, one interesting stone, an arch-stone of the Norman period, with a double moulding, zigzag and cable. Now there is no part of the present church to which this stone can be referred, though there is a great peculiarity about the chancel, which may lead to some theory........It might be worth while to see whether this moulding exists in Moyses' Hall."

With the reign of Stephen, the Jewish troubles in this country commenced, and the remnant of the scattered and sacred race settled in East Anglia, came in for a terrible share of those troubles. The bitter revengeful feelings which had been pent up during the reigns of the first three Norman kings, were now let loose, and raged with impetuous fury. The Christians of East Anglia must be credited with the fabrication of the foulest calumny ever coined against their Jewish neighbours, which proved most disastrous to the latter. In the ninth year of that reign, the Jews were, for the first time, accused of the crime of crucifying a Christian infant, William by name. The alleged cruel murder was said to have been perpetrated at Norwich. It was the inauguration of a long series of such allegations, in the various countries where the Jews were dispersed, against whom, for a time, sympathy had been permitted to become steeled, and for whose rights justice had been deprived of balances.

It may not be considered irrelevant if I state here the various and extraordinary reasons which the Gentile converts had invented to account for the flagrant calumny against the Jews. Some asserted that the scattered nation required Christian blood for the celebration of the Passover, ignorant of the Jewish law that a dead body renders a whole neighbourhood defiled. Others affirmed that the Hebrews required Christian blood to put it into their unleavened bread on the above-named festival, forgetful that blood was strictly prohibited in the law of Moses. It was also gravely stated that the Israelites used Christian blood

for personal deodorization. Others seasoned the charge with a spice of sensational romance Forsooth, the Jews wanted Christian blood to make love potions. Others maintained that with Christian blood the Jews stopped the bleeding of their infant sons, induced by the administration of the Abrahamic covenant seal. Some mysteriously stated that Christian blood was used at the celebration of Jewish weddings. Others vehemently asserted that the Jewish priests were obliged to have their hands tinged with it when they pronounced the Aaronic benediction in the synagogues. Others again asserted that the members of the synagogue used Christian blood to make their sacrifices acceptable. The most common story, however, was that Christian blood was used for the purpose of anointing dying Jews; that at the point of death, the rabbi anointed his departing brother, and secretly whispered into his ear the following words:—
"If the Messiah, on whom the Christians believe, be the promised true Messiah, may the blood of this innocent murdered Christian help thee to eternal life." Pierius Valerianus assures us "that the Jews purchase at a dear rate the blood of Christians, in order to raise devils, and that by making it boil, they obtained answers to all their questions." Such was the profound knowledge, of Jews and Judaism, which the Christians of East Anglia possessed in bygone days. Something akin to the knowledge which the ignorant peasantry of Spain possess of the English now-a-day, who have lately accused a British Consul of eating their children, which accusation nearly cost the Englishman his life.

During the reign of Henry II., it transpired that the ecclesiastics were already debtors to the Jews, and they therefore began to charge their creditors with usury, which was on all occasions held up, by the clergy, as a crime of the greatest magnitude. Had the ecclesiastics been really impressed by this belief, they should not, for the sake of moral consistency, have resorted to such sinners when they wanted money. Yet we learn that bishops, abbots, and monks of those days, pledged with the Jews the sacred vessels of their churches. In the records of this reign, we find it stated in connection with the Abbey of Bury St. Edmund's, amongst other things, that Isaac, the son of Rabbi Jocee, held a security for three hundred pounds. Benedict, the Jew of Norwich, held a security for eight hundred and fourscore pounds, which debt originated in a loan for rebuilding the parlour of the Abbacy, which was destroyed by fire. Another Jew, Jurnet by name, held security for sixty pounds. We also have it recorded, that a Jew of Bury St. Edmund's, Sancto by name—I wish that name to be borne in mind—was fined five marks for taking, as security for a loan, from the monks of that place, certain vessels dedicated to the service of the altar. Another Jew of Suffolk, Bennet by name—Bennet was a common Jewish name, I have never yet met a man of that name, who was not marked with strong characteristic Jewish features—was fined twenty pounds for taking some consecrated vestments as security. A curious story is related by Brompton, a monkish chronicler of the twelfth century, respecting William de Waterville, Abbot of Peterborough. That dignitary was deposed for having entered the abbey, at the head of a band of armed men, and having taken thence the arm of St. Oswald, the martyr, in order to pawn it to the Jews.* One of the claims advanced by Henry II. against Archbishop Thomas à Becket, was in reference to a sum of £500, for which that prince had been security for the primate to a Jew.

It is a faithful picture of the English of those days, " that when churchmen and laymen, prince and prior, knight and priest, come knocking at Isaac's door, they borrow not his shekels with these uncivil terms. It is then, Friend Isaac, will you pleasure us in this matter, and our day shall be truly kept, so God save me—and

---

* It is problematical whether the Jews would have advanced much upon that withered arm, but in the eyes of the members of the abbacy it was of great value, on account of its healing virtues. At the dissolution of the Abbey of Bury St. Edmund's, these relics, which the monks had in great esteem, were found, viz. : the sacred remains of King Edmund, enshrined ; the same king's shirt, entire ; certain drops of St. Stephen's blood, which were shed out of his body when he was stoned ; some of the coals on which St. Lawrence was broiled ; certain parings of the flesh of divers holy virgins ; a sinew of St. Edmund in a box ; several skulls of ancient saints and martyrs—among which was that of St. Petronill, which the people believed would cure all the diseases of the head by applying it to the aching part ; St. Edmund's sword, and St. Thomas of Canterbury's boots ; St. Botolph's bones in a coffin, which the monks made the people believe would procure rain when carried in procession in a time of drought ; certain wax candles, which being carried lighted round their corn-fields in seed-time, no darnel, tares, or any noisome weeds would grow among the corn that year ; with many others which, by the relation of the monks, would work wonderful effects.

kind Isaac, if ever you served a man, show yourself a friend in this need. And when the day comes and I ask my own, then what hear I, but the curse of Egypt on your tribe, and all that may stir up the rude and uncivil populace against poor strangers."*

The king and the priests, however, very often adopted a different mode from borrowing, when they stood in need of money. For instance, in the year 1179, when both the royal exchequer and the treasury of the Abbacy of Bury St. Edmund's were at their lowest ebb, from natural causes, the Jews of that town were all of a sudden charged with the unnatural crime of crucifying a boy, Robert by name, which device proved an important revenue both to the king and the abbot. The former took advantage of the supposed crime, and banished the wealthiest Jews of Bury St. Edmund's out of the country; and, as a matter of course, confiscated their properties. Those Jews he allowed to remain in the place, he fined very heavily. The abbot and the monks, on the other hand, caused a body of a child to be interred, as that of a martyred saint, with great ceremony and every mark of respect; the shrine was declared capable of producing supernatural effects, and it speedily became renowned for the miracles it wrought. Persons from all parts, led either by curiosity or credulity, visited the shrine. The offerings which were made on the occasion proved a most yielding mine of wealth.

The inauguration of the reign of Richard I. was the

* Sir Walter Scott.

ushering in of a new series of spoliations and murders, by British Christians, of Anglo-Hebrews; and the poor Jews who lived in East Anglia suffered as much as those who resided in any other place in this kingdom, except York. In the spring of 1190, when Richard had passed over to the continent, to join the king of France in the crusade to Palestine, and whilst the soldiers of the cross were preparing to follow him, "the people," using the words of a quaint old historian of Suffolk, "almost with one accord, through the whole nation, as if they had been summoned by a bell, fell upon the Jews, and slew many of them; and among other places such as inhabited Bury St. Edmund's were set upon, March 17, 1190, and many of them were slain, and the residue that escaped through the procurement of the abbot, named Sampson, were expelled the town.

Neither Jocelin of Brakelond, the contemporary monkish chronicler, nor his recent translator and editor, Mr. T. E. Tomlins, seem to me to have apprehended the real motives of Abbot Sampson, on the occasion. I believe those motives were of a humane and Christian character. The Jews and the heads of the Abbacy of Bury St. Edmund's had hitherto lived on very amicable terms. Brakelond, who was a thorough hater of his Saviour's kinsfolk, thus once introduced the latter into his chronicles. "The Jews, I say, to whom the sacrist [William] was said to be a father and protector, whose protection they indeed enjoyed, having free ingress and egress, and going all over the monastery, rambling about the altars and by the shrine, while high mass was being celebrated. Moreover, their monies were kept safe in our treasury, under the care of the sacrist, and what was still more improper, their wives with their little ones, were lodged in our pitancery in time of war." Now, Abbot Sampson was a just and upright man—of a different spirit from his pupil and biographer—he was determined therefore to secure the right of protecting the Jews of his town, " he alleging that whatsoever is within the town of St. Edmund, or within the liberties thereof, of right belongeth to St. Edmund. Therefore the Jews ought to become the men of St. Edmund's." The king naturally demurred to the claim; by acquiescing he would not only have established a precedent upon which all the other monasteries, where the Jews resided, would have been ready to act, but he would have lost his great gold-mine. The demand was therefore negatived. Sampson, who evidently took no pleasure in the sport of persecuting the Jews under his very eyes, demanded permission to expel them altogether from his town. The license was readily granted to the determined abbot. He took care, however, that the exiles " had all their chattels, and the value of their houses and lands." That no evil might befall them on their way to the divers towns where they were going to, armed forces were ordered to protect them. It was also provided, that "if the Jews should come to the great pleas of the abbot to demand their debts from their debtors, on such occasions they might for two days and two nights lodge within the town, and on the third day be permitted to depart without injury." So far, there is no evidence of malevolent hostility on the part of that abbot towards the Jews of Bury St. Edmund's. Was Sampson—the name bewrayeth him—a descendant of those Hebrews who professed the whole of the Jewish religion—an " Israelite indeed ?"*

The Jews of Cambridge, Norwich, and Lynn, suffered similar outrages of rapine and murder. It must be owned that the Jews of Lynn were themselves the authors of their sufferings then. A member of their own community saw cogent reasons to admit the second part of the Jewish faith, namely, the full development of that religion as revealed in the New Testament. The unbelievers in that part of their religion saw proper to take vengeance upon the believer. They waylaid him, and one day, as he passed through a certain street, they were determined to get him into their power. He made his escape to

---

* His personal appearance, as well as his character, seems to favour the supposition. Jocelin of Brakelond describes him " of middle stature, having an oval face, a prominent nose, thick lips, clear and very piercing eyes, ears of nicest sense of hearing, lofty eyebrows . . . . having a few grey hairs in his reddish beard, with a few grey in a black head of hair, which somewhat curled . . . . a man remarkably temperate, never slothful, well able and willing to ride or walk till old age came upon him and moderated such inclination." Respecting the abbot's kinsmen, the same chronicler says, "He had not, or assumed not to have had any relative within the third degree. But I have heard him state, that he had relations who were noble and gentle, whom he never would in any wise recognise as relations; for, as he said, they would be more a burden than an honour to him, if they should happen to find out their relationship."

a neighbouring church, to which he was pursued by some of the Jewish persecutors. Whereupon some sailors belonging to a ship lying in the harbour raised a cry that the unbelievers intended to put the believer to death. The sailors were joined by the townspeople, under the plea of saving the life of the persecuted one, drove the persecutors to their houses, and then followed themselves, murdered the would-be murderers, carried off whatever valuables they could find, and then set fire to the rifled houses. The sailors, enriched by the spoil, embarked immediately on board their vessel, set sail, and got clear off.*

It was aptly said of the Anglo-Hebrews of those days, by a French historian, that they were used as sponges, allowed for a time to absorb a large amount of wealth, which, when filled, were wrung out into the coffers of the crown. As an illustration of the pertinency of the simile may be adduced the first few years of King John's reign. As soon as that monarch succeeded to the throne he began by giving all sorts of encouragement to the devoted race; he not only permitted the exiles to return to the towns and homes from which they were banished, and granted charters in their favour,† but he also threw out baits for foreign Jews, in order to lure them to take up their residence in this country. The synagogues in East Anglia—that of Bury St. Edmund's included—were re-opened. Again three times a day—morning, noon, and evening—were they attended by Jewish worshippers.

* See Appendix E.   † See Appendix F.

But as soon as his majesty perceived that his human sponges were sufficiently filled out, he began to wring them with a fierce tenacity, with a cruel grasp, with a murderous grip, that only John was capable of. Many a Jew was tortured to death, in order to discover his supposed riches; whilst many more were thrown into dungeons for the same purpose.

That sovereign's Gentile subjects must also have felt severely the effects of that remorseless pressure, as may be inferred from the 12th and 13th clauses in the Magna Charta—which instrument, by the bye, was drawn up at Bury St. Edmund's—they are the following: "If any one have borrowed anything of the Jews, more or less, and died before the debt be satisfied, there shall no interest be paid for that debt, so long as the heir is under age, of whomsoever he will hold; and if the debt fall into our hands, we will take only the chattel mentioned in the charter or instrument. If any one shall be indebted to the Jews, his wife shall have her dower, and pay nothing for the debt; and if the deceased leave children under age, they shall have necessaries provided for them according to the tenements of the deceased, and out of the residue the debts shall be paid, saving however the service of the Lord."

On the death of John, the Jews experienced an interval of respite from persecution, on the part of the state. Happily, the government of the country, during the minority of Henry III, fell successively into the hands of men of distinguished ability and virtue.

As soon as the Earl of Pembroke entered upon his exalted office, as guardian to the youthful King, he adopted measures for the special relief and protection of the persecuted Anglo-Hebrews. Many individuals amongst them were exonerated from the burdens which had been previously imposed upon them; and numbers were immediately liberated from imprisonments, to which, upon various pretences, they had, under the late King, been condemned. Writs and letters patent were issued, directed to the principal burgesses of each of the towns where the Jews resided, commanding that they should be held secure from any injuries, both as to their persons and their properties; and particularly that they should be guarded against any violence from the hands of the crusaders. In addition to these measures, a confirmation of the charter, which the Anglo-Hebrews had obtained in the beginning of the late reign, was granted; by the terms of which most important privileges were accorded to them, and their persons and estates were shielded from violence. At the same time, with the confirmation of their former charter, the Jews were further exempted from the jurisdiction of the ecclesiastical courts.

Hubert de Burgh who, upon the death of the Earl of Pembroke, succeeded to the administration of the government, continued his predecessor's humane deportment towards the Anglo-Hebrews. During the fifteen years that those ministers, respectively, wielded the sceptre of this land, no instances are recorded of any acts of violence having been committed against the Jews. On the contrary, we are informed that many unlooked-for privileges were lavished upon them.

The protection thus extended to the remnant of the scattered nation in this land, again inspired them with confidence; those who had survived the atrocious oppressions of the last reign, began once more to accumulate wealth; and numbers of their co-religionists were induced once more to come over from the continent, and settle in this country.

The clergy, it would seem, took umbrage at the privileges which the Jews enjoyed, and resolved to attempt, by an exercise of ecclesiastical authority, to counteract the effects of the protection which had been afforded by the measures of the government. Stephen Langton, Archbishop of Canterbury, in conjunction with Hugo de Velles, Bishop of Lincoln, published a general prohibition, by which all persons were forbidden to buy anything of the Jews, or sell them any victuals or necessaries, or to have any communication with them. The primate, moreover, promulgated at his provincial synod the following edict:—

"That the Jews do not keep Christian servants; and let the servants be compelled by ecclesiastical censure to observe this, and the Jews by canonical punishments, or by some extraordinary penalty contrived by the diocesan. Let them not be permitted to build any more synagogues, but be looked upon as debtors to the churches of the parishes where they reside, as to tithes and offerings.

" To prevent, moreover, the intimacy of Jewish men and women with Christians of either sex, we charge by the authority of the General Council, that the Jews of both sexes wear a linen cloth, two inches broad and four fingers long, of a different colour from their own clothes, on their upper garment, before their breast; and that they be compelled to do this by ecclesiastical censure; and let them not presume to enter into any Church."

The Jews appealed to the Crown for protection, and obtained relief. Directions were sent to the sheriffs of the different counties and cities, to prevent the prohibitions being enforced; and orders were given to imprison all persons who, by reason of the commands of the Church, refused to sell provisions to the Jews.

When Henry III., at the age of sixteen, in the year 1223, assumed the reins of the government himself, the conduct of public affairs appeared under a different aspect. From henceforth the Jews, in place of the security which they had previously enjoyed, were subjected to ceaseless violence and arbitrary exactions. This monarch began by seizing the whole of the property of any Jew who admitted the divine character of the Judaism proclaimed from Calvary, as well as that from Sinai, and thus joined the Christian Church. It is a pleasing consideration, that notwithstanding such cruel anti-Christian conduct, on the part of a nominal Christian king, there were Anglo-Hebrews of great celebrity who hazarded everything in obedience to conviction and conscience, and became Israelites indeed. Those thorough-going Jews I am not disposed to pity; they counted the cost of their confessing the faith, and gloried in the bargain which they had made. But those Jews who were neither convinced nor conscious of the incompleteness of their Judaism are to be pitied by every feeling heart. Scarcely a year in the long reign of Henry III. was allowed to pass without heavy taxes, to an enormous amount, being exacted from the Anglo-Hebrews. Those taxes were enforced by imprisonment, by seizure of property, and the persons of wives and children. Punctuality of payment was secured by compelling the richest Jews to become securities for their respective communities, under the above-named penalties.

In the year 1232, the king having taxed the anti-Christian Jews to the amount of 18,000 marks, and having robbed the Christian Jews of their all, his majesty was moved, it is said, by the wailing and gnashing of teeth, which the purgatorial fire wrung from his tormented sire—the most cruel oppressor of his Jewish subjects—determined on establishing a home for those Jews who sacrificed everything to their convictions of the divine character of the New Testament, where they had board, lodgings, and the means of instruction.* Be it known, however, that the king was no loser by the establishment—the house itself was, on some pretext, taken from a Jew, John Herberton by name—and he took care to indemnify him-

* See Appendix G.

self more than enough by the exorbitant imposts which he put upon the Jewish community from time to time. In these days, when the spoils of the old times are being restored to the representatives of the spoiled, and when Hebrew-Christians are being daily added to the Church, it would be but an honest act to restore the property, under trustees, to the representatives of the Anglo-Hebrew Christians of former days.*

The Jews of East Anglia were at that time exceedingly rich, and suffered proportionately whenever the king was in need of money. As an illustration, let me name the year 1235—the year in which Henry spent a great deal on his sister Isabella's marriage to the Emperor of Germany, as well as on his own contemplated marriage with Eleanor of Provence. Seven of the most opulent Jews of Norwich were accused of circumcising a little boy of that city. The accused were brought before the king himself, whilst he was celebrating his nativity at Westminster. The poor Jews were condemned to be drawn and hanged, and, of course, their property to be confiscated; and thus were the king's wants supplied for that time. That charge, of circumcising little Gentile boys, against the Jews, became a source of lucrative income to the needy Church and State of that period. One of the most famous mock trials of that reign took place in 1240, when a very rich Jew of the city of Norwich, Jacob by name, was accused of stealing a small Gen-

* See Appendix H.

tile boy from his parents and circumcising him. I cannot enter here into a detailed account of that *cause celebre.** Sufficient to say, that after the case for the prosecution had ominously broken down, notwithstanding the hard perjury of certain witnesses, four very opulent Jews were condemned to be dragged by horses' tails, and then hanged. The populace who, as usual, waited for an opportunity to rob and plunder, set fire to the houses of the Jews, and reduced them to ashes. So barefaced were those murderers and robbers, that when the sheriff of Norfolk ventured to interfere on behalf of the sufferers, they complained to the king of the sheriff's interposition.

In the very next year the Anglo-Hebrew communities throughout the kingdom were startled by writs to elect a certain number out of their respective congregations, to meet the king at a Parliament at Worcester, in order, as the writs ran, "to treat with the king both concerning his own and their benefit." Many of the oppressed people began to entertain sanguine hopes that the king was about to pass a "gracious and generous" measure in their behalf; but to their dismay they soon found that the bill which the king proposed was "severe and sweeping," in other words, it was a bill of "pains and penalties." The purport of his majesty's most gracious preamble was that the king wanted money, and that of the bill that the Jews must raise him twenty thousand marks. That convention is called by the chroniclers of the time *Parliamentum Judaicum.* East Anglia furnished

* See Appendix I.

nine representatives to that singular Parliament; namely, Cambridge six, Isaac ben Samuel, Jacob ben Deusestra, Aaron ben Isaac Blund, Josce de Wilton, Dyaye ben Rabbi, Levi ben Solomon; and Norwich three, Henne Jurninius ben Jacob, Deucrese ben Dyaya de Manecroft, and Dure de Resing. The other Jewish communities in East Anglia must have dwindled away by this, both as regards numbers and wealth, and were not in a position to send deputies to that extraordinary Parliament. A melancholy monotony, as regards the Anglo-Hebrews, pervaded the fifty years' English history after that Parliament, when the sacred unmixed race were finally banished from this then inhospitable country, by the mixed races who subjugated it. The history of the Anglo-Hebrews, during the last jubilee of their residence in Britain, may be summed up in three words—robbery, torture, and murder; varied now and then in the ferocious barbarity of the inhuman robbers and murderers.

As has been hinted, the Anglo-Hebrews, the oldest settlers in this island, were ruthlessly banished from this country in 1290. The expulsion was accompanied by atrocities on the part of the banishers— the comparatively new settlers—the thoughts of which make one's blood run cold.

Very scanty indeed are the vestiges of the historic Anglo-Hebrews in this realm. Antiquarians and archæologists have now and then brought to light some fragments belonging to some monuments of the ante-expulsion Jews, which though comparatively trifling in themselves, are yet endowed with solemn interest to the thoughtful student of Jewish history. It is difficult now to point out clearly the ancient Hebrew houses, whether public or private; for though Edward I. ordered a strict inventory to be made of all the Jewish estates, with the design, as he promised, to convert them all to pious purposes, yet nothing was more remote from his royal intentions. The inventory was indeed made, and an auction too, but the proceeds were converted to anything but pious purposes. The English Justinian squandered away the money in a most reprehensible manner, without a single penny having been applied to those pious uses of which the devout king talked. Whole rolls full of patents relative to Jewish estates are still to be seen in the archives of the metropolis, which estates, together with their rents in fee, pensions, and mortgages, were all seized by the king. Besides those Jewish records on parchment, there are some in stone, namely, a few Christian churches which were formerly Jewish synagogues; also some streets and walks, which are distinguished by the names of Jewry, Jews' Way, Jews' Walk, Jewin Street, Jews' Wall, Jews' Mount, &c., &c.

One of the most interesting reliques of the historic Anglo-Hebrews, in pretty good preservation, is found in the town of Bury St. Edmund's, namely the present police station.* It was known by its original

* A considerable portion of the east end of the original building was cut off about a century ago, to widen a lane or street. For further particulars, see Appendix J.

possessors and founders as קהלת משה, "the Synagogue of Moses." It was, no doubt, a Jewish place of worship, and so named, either because it was dedicated to the service of Almighty God, as prescribed by Israel's deliverer from Egypt, or because the founder was an Anglo-Hebrew whose name was Moses. The modern Jewish synagogue at Ramsgate was founded by a Jewish baronet, well known for his extensive philanthropy, and goes amongst the Jews by the name of "Sir Moses' Synagogue."

On examining the one at Bury St. Edmund's, I found it to correspond, in its architectural details, with the oldest existing synagogue in Europe, that of Prague. The rabbi's, or the founder's house—probably the founder was one of the early rabbis of the Bury St. Edmund's Synagogue—was not only contiguous to it, but communicated with the synagogue. After a careful survey of the adjoining places, I have come to the conclusion that the whole of the south side of the square of the market-place belonged to the synagogue establishment, and premises; including seminary, official residences, baptistries, &c., &c.—in fact, a sort of Hebrew abbacy of Bury St. Edmund's. According to the Jewish ritual males and females have to perform, at sundry times, certain ablutions by immersion. Every synagogue is provided therefore with baptistries, in its immediate vicinity, for that purpose. I happened to visit the synagogue of Rotterdam in the course of last year, and four such baptistries were pointed out to me. On examining the premises adjoining the police station at Bury St. Edmund's, I found an old well, which was evidently one of the baptistries, as well as traces of others, plainly vestiges of their primitive Jewish use.

The synagogue proper consisted of the ground floor; the centre was occupied by the בימה, "Bimah," a square raised platform where the law was read on Sabbaths, feasts, festivals, Mondays, and Thursdays; the east end was dedicated as the ark, in which the scrolls of the Pentateuch were deposited, in front of which was a raised platform, for the Aaronites to stand upon on certain grand festivals, when it is their office to pronounce the sacerdotal benediction, as prescribed in Numb. vi. 23—26. From that platform was also delivered an occasional discourse. In front stood the nine-branched candlestick, for the celebration of "the Feast of Dedication."* There was a niche by the side of the ark, in which was placed a lamp, ever burning, in accordance with Levit. xxiv. 1—4. The west end, below the "Bimah" was apportioned to stran-

* A festive anniversary, under the name of חנכה, or "Dedication," has been ordained in the house of Israel, by Judas Maccabæus, to commemorate the inauguration of the Temple which was restored by him. To the present time, throughout the Jewish world, this festival is observed for eight days, beginning with the 25th of the ninth month; which generally falls about the end of December. The great feature of the commemoration is the ceremonial of lighting lamps or candles in the following manner, immediately after sunset, for eight successive evenings:—The first night one lamp or candle is lighted; the second night two; the third night three; and so on, till the eighth night. In most synagogues there is a nine-branched candlestick for the purpose, the ninth light, or lamp, serving as the illuminator of the respective one, two, three, &c.

gers and mourners; the rest was occupied by the regular male members of the congregation. Beyond the west end arches there must have been an ante-room, or portico, which contained the laver, the different alms' chests, &c. Over the portico there must have been a latticed gallery, to ascend which a staircase would be required, for the female members of the community. The floors of the synagogues of Orthodox Jews were considerably below the level of ordinary houses, to which the worshippers descended by a flight of steps, conformably to Psalm cxxx., which begins with the words, "Out of the depths have I cried unto Thee, O Lord!" The synagogue under review must have been very deep; it evidently had no windows. Be it remembered that the historic Anglo-Hebrews had been often prohibited, under severe pains and penalties, making their supplications audible, lest the sensitive ears of the Gentile Christians of those days should be irritated. This synagogue must have been illuminated by day, as well as by night, by artificial light.

There ought to be also traces of a tower, from whence the moon, at a certain age, was monthly apostrophised in the form of a short service. In the places where the Jews are numerous, that monthly service is solemnised out of doors, when the moon is between seven and fifteen days old.*

* Since the above was written, my attention has been directed to Mr. Hudson Turner's "Domestic Architecture of the Middle Ages," and Mr. Tymms' "Hand-book of Bury St. Edmund's," which works indirectly confirm the opinions I have formed from personal observations. See Appendix J.

In connection with this archæological specimen in stone, I have to bring under your notice another one in bronze, which I believe to have been one of the vessels which once belonged to the synagogue of Bury St. Edmund's. I regret very much that it is out of my power to exhibit the relic itself, but I venture to hope that Lady Pigot's drawing of it, enlarged from a small pen and ink sketch preserved amongst the MSS. in the British Museum,* and my humble description of it, will give some idea of its character and probable use. I ought to tell you that her ladyship's drawing is considerably larger than the original vessel was; the latter measured eight quarts.

About two hundred years ago, as a fisherman was dragging a brook in the county of Suffolk, probably the Lark, he nearly broke his net by some heavy capture. On landing it, he discovered that he had fished up a curious vessel, upon three legs, which had on its outside cincture certain characters which were Greek to him. Let me in the first place state the reason why I think that the vessel was found in the immediate vicinity of Bury St. Edmund's. When the fisherman secured his prize, he sold it immediately to the Rev. Dr. John Covell, then Master of Christ's College, Cambridge. Now, Dr. Covell was a native of Horningsheath, or Horringer, and educated in the Grammar School of Bury St. Edmund's. He often visited the places in which he was born and bred, whenever vacation from his various duties afforded him an opportunity to do so. I do not think that I am wrong in sup-

* See Frontispiece.

posing that the vessel was found and bought on one of the doctor's visits to this neighbourhood.

The acquisition proved a very perplexing study to the Master of Christ's College. He knew sufficient of the Hebrew alphabet to be aware that the inscription on the cincture of his purchase was not Greek. For all that, the inscription was a most inexplicable philological problem to the purchaser. His own University seemed, at that time, destitute of a single Hebrew scholar who could help him to a solution of his problem. I find among the MSS. in the British Museum two letters addressed to Dr. Covell, evidently in answer to queries about that very vessel; one by the then Marquis of Northampton, who was a dabbler in Hebrew antiquities, and another by a Mr. Isaac Abendana, a learned Jew of Oxford. But as the doctor would not trust the vessel out of his keeping, and as his delineation of it, and its inscription, was far from lucid, his correspondents' conjectures were anything but enlightening. With them I will not trespass upon the attention of my indulgent audience at present; their proper positions are as footnotes or appendices.*

At the doctor's death, in 1722, the vessel was purchased by the then Earl of Oxford. His lordship did—according to the light which he possessed—the proper thing; he sent the vessel to Oxford, in order to have the inscription deciphered and explained by Mr. John Gagnier, the Professor of Oriental

* See Appendix K.

Languages in that University.* We are indebted to that Orientalist for a tolerable copy of the letters of the inscription, but we owe him nothing either for his grouping, or for the explanation of the same; they only serve, as circumstantial evidence, to prove how little knowledge of eastern languages was then required from a Gentile Professor of Oriental Literature. I am pleased to think that there are several Hebrew scholars amongst my hearers,† I shall therefore read the inscription, in the first instance, in the original. For the large diagram of the inscription, I am also indebted to Lady Pigot's skill in Hebrew caligraphy. It consists, as you must perceive, of the names concerned, the principal personage being described in two rhymed couplets, one short and one long, and closes with a line which explains the object of the vessel.

הנדר

יוסף בן הק'ר' יחיאל

ז'צ'ק'ל'

המשיב ושואל

לקהל כהואל

כדי לחזות פני אריאל

בכתב דת יקותיאל

וצדקה תציל ממות:

---

* Mr. Gagnier was a Frenchman, which may account for his ingeniously improvising the name of a town, in default of knowing the meaning of certain Hebrew words. (See Appendix L.)

† Lord Arthur Hervey, the present Bishop of Bath and Wells,

Of which the following is a literal translation:—

"The offerer is Joseph, the son of Rabbi Yechiel Sancto, (the memory of a righteous man, who is holy, is to be blessed,) who answered and questioned the congregation as he thought proper. That he may behold the face of Ariel, with the writing DATH YEKUTHIEL. And may righteousness deliver from death."

I must trouble you with a few annotations ere I make the purport of the inscription intelligible. First about Rabbi Yechiel Sancto. קדוש, or Sancto, was evidently a family surname, and of old standing at Bury St. Edmund's. It will be remembered that in an earlier part of this paper, an individual of that name was mentioned as having been fined for taking the sacred vessels of the abbey as security for a loan.* Rabbi Yechiel is a well-known name in the Talmudical literature of the middle ages, and frequently quoted in the addenda to the Talmud, termed TOSEPHOTH. The Rabbi Yechiel named in the inscription, I consider to have been one of the later rabbis of the synagogue of Bury St. Edmund's, as the first couplet,

"Who answered and questioned
The congregation as he thought proper,"

evidently implies. This rabbi was the author of a work on the Pentateuch, under the title of DATH

occupied the chair when the paper was read, and there were, besides, several other Hebrew Scholars amongst the audience.
* See p. 27.

YEKUTHIEL, or "the Law of Yekuthiel"—Yekuthiel being a name by which Moses is known in Rabbinical writings. With the MS. of that work the author was determined to undertake a pilgrimage to Jerusalem, to submit it to the Masters of his people in the Holy City—not an uncommon occurrence in the middle ages—which I clearly discern in the second couplet,

"That he may behold the face of Ariel,*
With the writing of Dath Yekuthiel."†

That is, that the pious pilgrim may enjoy a safe

* Ariel is a term used for Jerusalem. See Isaiah xxix. 1.

† The words כהואל and יקותיאל occur in a couplet, being part of a poem recited in the synagogue, on the Festival of the Law, called שמחת תורה. The couplet runs thus:—

יה שבת ממפעל כהואל
ויקדש שביעי כבכתב יקותיאל:

"*Yah* rested from work as He deemed proper,
And sanctified the seventh day, as [it is recorded] in the writing of *Yekuthiel*.

A work under the title of דת יקותיאל, the burden of which was an exposition of the 613 precepts, supposed to be inculcated in the Pentateuch, was actually published in 1696, (by a strange coincidence, the very year in which the vessel was discovered,) at Zolkiew, by Süskind ben Solomon Yekuthiel. Whether the published work was an original one, or an appropriation of the work of our Rabbi Yechiel, will remain a problem. The latter supposition is not without instances in the history of Hebrew works. An example of it was afforded in this country, when a certain Jew published a Hebrew Commentary on one of the Prophets, under his own name, which was the work of an author long since dead and buried, and little known to Biblical students in England—no, not even to the well-read Mr. Zedner, late of the British Museum, who was betrayed to father the work upon the plagiarist.

and prosperous journey and attain his object, his son Joseph made the offering of that vessel to the synagogue of which his father was chief. But for what use or purpose was that vessel intended? The last line answers the question,—

"And righteousness delivereth from death;"

which, with the post-Biblical Jews, means "Almsgiving delivereth from death." * Such is the inscription on every alms' receptacle to be found in the porticos of every well-ordered synagogue. I have noticed last year, in the course of a continental tour, that inscription on the vessels placed in the porticos of the synagogues, for the reception of alms. This vessel, therefore, I conclude was placed in the portico of the synagogue of Bury St. Edmund's, for the reception of votive offerings from the members of the congregation, for the safety of their pilgrim rabbi; which offerings were intended to be forwarded for the benefit of the poor Jewish saints at Jerusalem. When the banishment of the then Anglo-Hebrews took place, the unhappy exiles either buried or sunk in rivers and brooks many of their valuables and sacred things, that the articles might not fall into the hands of the rapacious Anglo-Gentiles. Hence the finding of that vessel in a Suffolk river. The lid which belonged to it has never been heard of as yet. Time may yet bring both to light.

I am, moreover, led to conjecture that the expulsion

* For Professor Gagnier's interpretation, as given by Tovey, see Appendix L.

of the Jews from this country took place between that rabbi's departure for Jerusalem and his return to Europe. On reaching the latter, he had learnt the calamity which had befallen his people in England, and after spending some time in Paris, where he disputed with a certain Hebrew Christian, Nicolaus by name, whom I shall presently introduce, he took up his abode at Prague, where his family had probably taken refuge. He, and his posterity after him, whilst preserving the name Yechiel, assumed the surname "Yerushalmy," that is, De Jerusalem. On examining some of the epitaphs in the ancient Jewish cemetery of Prague, I found one which marks the burying-place of a Rabbi Yechiel ben Joseph De Jerusalem, dated 1598. The late Chief Rabbi of Prague, Solomon Jehudah Rappoport, a man of vast antiquarian learning, remarked in his Hebrew biographical essay, on some of the celebrities whose remains rest in that cemetery, that Rabbi Yechiel was descended from a very ancient Jewish family, whose ancestor came from Jerusalem a long time ago, and settled at Prague. Many of his descendants are even now men of mark. One of his scions was ennobled by the late Emperor of Austria, and assumed the name of Baron Salemfels.

Let me just mention the vicissitudes of the Suffolk vessel, as far as I could trace it. My young friend, Mr. Arthur Pigot, put a query respecting its whereabouts in the "Notes and Queries." The question elicited the answer that "at the dispersion of the antiquities belonging to Edward, Earl of Oxford, on March 8, 1741—2, there was a bell metal Jewish vessel upon three legs, purchased by Rawlinson for £1 5s." Another friend, Mr. Bernal Osborne, who takes an interest in the discovery of the vessel, wrote to me a short time ago, " I have seen Sir Christopher Rawlinson, who is a descendant of the antiquary in whose possession the bronze vessel was traced. It appears some of the effects of this Dr. Rawlinson were sold at his death, but he left his pictures, books, MSS., to St. John's College, Oxford. Whether the vessel was sold or left to the college, I could not ascertain." Probably one of the results of this meeting may prove the discovery, if it still exists anywhere, of that most interesting relic of the historic Anglo-Hebrews of East Anglia.*

Besides those vestiges of the scattered nation amongst you in bygone days, in stone and brass, there are vast numbers in flesh and blood. Strange as it may sound, it is yet true, notwithstanding the twofold persecution to which the " Israelite indeed " was subjected, on his repenting of his former rejection of the second part of Judaism, and accepting the dictum of the Deliverer greater than Moses ; I say, notwithstanding the double persecution which awaited those Nathanaels—the loss of all things to the king, and the loss of personal safety amongst his brethren after the flesh—many members of the historic Anglo-Hebrews' synagogues courageously braved, with Pauline fortitude, every danger, and boldly maintained that Christ was the end of the law for righteousness to every one

* See Postscript.

that believeth. Considerable numbers, on the other hand, joined the Church to save themselves from a dire and dreary exile, when the edict of expulsion was about to be put into effect. I trace the descendants of those historic Anglo-Hebrews in the names and physiognomies of the so-called "true-born Englishmen." I see vestiges of them in every assembly I have an opportunity of observing. Others may think what they please; but I consider that it is an infinitely higher honour—I mean for people who seek honour one from another, in consideration of pedigree—to be able to trace one's descent, be it ever so remotely, to the sacred race, than to the equivocal races of Saxon, Dane, Norman, Batavian, &c., &c. De Foe's satire has the sting of stern truth when he apostrophises the bragging Briton in the uncouth lines:—

"Thus from a mixture of all kinds began
That het'rogenous thing, an Englishman.
＊　＊　＊　＊　＊
Fate jumbled them together, God knows how;
Whate'er they were, they're true-born English now."

There is one name in particular amongst the historic Anglo-Hebrew believers in both covenants which deserves a passing notice. It is a name which once rang through the halls of learning all over Europe, during the transition of the Church from a deformed to a reformed state; a name which furnished opportunity for more than one Latin pun. It is the name of Nicolaus de Lyra. Both Roman Catholics and the early Protestants gave to that erudite and learned writer the credit of Luther's illumination. Pflug, Bishop of Naumberg, had improvised the couplet:

> "Si Lyra non lyrasset
> Lutherus non saltasset."

A Protestant scholar played upon the name to the same tune, but with a variation, and made the couplet run thus :—

> "Nisi Lyra lyrasset
> Totus mundus delirasset."

Wickliffe has also profited much by De Lyra's writings, he used them frequently when translating the Bible. Those writings were formerly very famous. Pope, in giving the catalogue of Bay's Library, in his "Dunciad," finds

> "De Lyra there a dreadful front extend."

I believe that I am in a position to solve a biographical problem which has hitherto defied those interested in such matters. I believe the celebrated "Israelite indeed" was an East Anglian, a native of Lynn. The writers of biographical dictionaries, copying one another, thus begin their sketch of that celebrity :—" So called from the place of his birth, Lyra in Normandy," &c., &c. I never could discover whether there is, or ever was, such a place as Lyra in Normandy; nor have the gazetteer makers and guide-book compilers succeeded in making the discovery. But what I did discover is this, that De Lyra himself, in the title-page of one of his works, gives England as his native country. There can be but one opinion, that he must have been better informed on this subject than his biographer L'Advocat—who lived about 500 years after De Lyra—who, because Nicolaus happened to have been at Paris for some time, and was known by the surname of De Lyra, made a Frenchman of the illustrious stranger.* Bishop Bale, himself a native of East Anglia, who flourished about a century after Nicolaus De Lyra—positively states that the great harbinger of the Reformation was an Anglo-Hebrew Christian.†

Now, I find in an old history of Norfolk, that about the same time that the great author I am speaking of flourished—*i.e.*, the latter part of the thirteenth and the first part of the fourteenth century—there flourished at Lynn a learned monk, who was a native of that town, and was known as Nicolaus of Lynn. That book tells me that that monk was a very learned man, a great scholar, a great divine, a great mathematician, an astronomer, and a great musician; that he was educated at Oxford, and that he belonged to the Franciscan order. Exactly the same is affirmed of Nicolaus de Lyra. If there were two such persons, then Oxford must have been the Alma Mater of remarkable twins, christened by the same name! I do not believe in the coincidence. There was only one

---

* The "Nouvelle Biographie Générale," published in 1860, is indeed circumstantial on the subject, the notice of the celebrity under review begins as follows:—"Lyra (Nicolas de) exégète théologien français, né vers 1270, à Lyra, bourg situé pres d'Evreux, mort a Paris, le 23 October, 1340." But who does not know the facility with which a certain class of French literati coin names. As an instance, see Appendix L.

† See Appendix M.

Nicolaus at Oxford, my "Israelite indeed," but he was one and the same with the Nicolaus of Lynn, and by reason of his musical proclivities, his friends and admirers turned De Lynn into De Lyra. I have no doubt in my own mind that the eminent Anglo-Hebrews I have just spoken of, namely Rabbi Yechiel and Father Nicolaus—the former an anti-Christian Jew, and the latter a Christian Jew—met at Paris towards the latter end of the thirteenth century, when a fierce theological dispute took place between them, the result of which was a small Hebrew volume by the unbelieving Jew, couched in the most intemperate and blasphemous language.*

De Lyra was not the only Jew of high attainments about that time, who found out that the law without the gospel was but Judaism unveiled. In the same century there flourished in Spain a Rabbi Solomon Halaywee, a native of Burgos, and founder of the cathedral in that place. He is known in ecclesiastical history by his baptismal name, as Pablo de Santa Maria, Bishop of Carthagena. A contemporary Spanish poet said of him "that he possessed all human learning, all the secrets of high philosophy; he was a masterly theologian, a sweet orator, an admirable historian, a clear and veracious narrator, one of whom every person spoke well. He continued—

"'Twas my delight to sit with him
Beneath the solemn ivy tree—

* It is preserved by Wagenseil in his *Tela Ignea Satanæ*. It shows of what spirit anti-Christian Jews are made, and how unchangeable is the hostility of the unbeliever towards the believer.

> To hide me from the sunny beam
> Beneath the laurel's shade, and see
> The little silver streamlet flowing :
> While from his lips a richer stream
> Fell, with the light of wisdom glowing—
> How sweet to slake my thirst with him!"

I cannot close this paper without remarking on the great change of feeling towards the sacred race in civilized Christendom. It was truly said by an eminent living Anglo-Hebrew, "In exact proportion as we have been favoured by nature, we have been persecuted by man. After a thousand struggles; after acts of heroic courage that Rome has never equalled; deeds of divine patriotism that Athens, and Sparta, and Carthage have never excelled; we have endured fifteen hundred years of supernatural slavery, during which every device that can degrade or destroy man has been the destiny that we have sustained and baffled."

Yes! baffled! the very sees, whose Archbishops and Bishops had once fulminated anathemas against the Anglo-Hebrews, are at this present moment filled by prelates nominated by an Anglo-Hebrew. The present Primate of all England, the Bishops of London, Lincoln, and Peterborough bear rule by the appointment of the ex-Prime Minister of England; and the present Prime Minister is beholden for his seat, in the House of Commons, to the superior influence of his colleague, a modern Anglo-Hebrew, David Salomons; and he who has had the honour to address you, and to whom you have listened with such patient indulgence, has the privilege to belong to the same race.

POSTSCRIPT.

AFTER the Paper had been read, approved of, and commended, a short discussion ensued, the principal burden of which was the disputing—on the part of the Rev. J. J. Raven, Head Master of Yarmouth Grammar School—the purpose of the bronze vessel (pp. 46—53.) as I described it. He resolutely maintained that he saw one like it, of about the same date, at the York Museum, with a Latin inscription, which purported that the vessel was intended as a mortar for compounding drugs, and he therefore conceived such to have been the use of the vessel which I described. In vain did I appeal to the purport of the Hebrew inscription of the vessel which I brought under notice, Mr. Raven clung to his conception with exemplary parental tenacity. However, our difference of opinion only tended to produce a cordial friendship between us. The following extracts from letters on the subject, which he has subsequently addressed to me, may be perused with interest, on account of the hints which they suggest.

Yarmouth, 29*th July,* 1869.

I am very desirous of tracing the history of the bronze vessel found in a Suffolk river, of which you produced a drawing at the meeting of the Royal Archæological Institute, at Bury, last week. Whether it be a receptacle for alms, according to your view, or a mortar for compounding drugs, according to mine, it is clearly amongst the earliest specimens of bronze-casting in England. I understood you to say that it was in the collection of the second Harley, Earl of Oxford, and that it may possibly be in the hands of the Pesident and Fellows of St. John's College, Oxford. When you elicit the truth as to this conjecture, I shall be greatly obliged if you will let me know. In the meanwhile I have a request to make, which I can only justify on the ground of my long and obscure labours in the history of bell-casting, &c.* It is, that you would let me have a copy, or tracing, of the smaller sketch of this vessel, which you exhibited, and of the inscription upon it. I think of having a photograph taken of the mortar in the York Museum, of which I spoke in the discussion after your paper, and I much wish to compare the outline, position of inscription, and general bearing of the two vessels. I fear that the vessel itself has perished. That at York was accidentally saved from the furnace in 1811, at Birmingham, by Rudder the bell-founder, and presented to Mr. Blunt, a surgeon in the town, whose collection was sold in 1835, when a Mr. Kenrick, of West Bromwich, bought it for a large sum, and presented it to the York Museum. The inscription on it is:—

MORTARIV̄ : SŌJ - TONĪS - EWANGEL
DE - IFIRMARJA - BE - MARIE - EBO.

And on the lower rim :—

FR - WILLS - DE - TOVTHORP - ME - FECIT - A.D. - M.CCC.VIII.

It weighs about 76 lbs., and stands, I should say, some 18 in. high. The history of the Harleian vessel may serve to connect the Anglo-Hebrews with the early history of founding in England. The only name of a founder discovered by me which has any hint of Jewish origin is *Symon de Hatfelde*, who appears

* Mr. Raven read a most interesting Essay on "The Church Bells of Cambridgeshire," on the same day that I read my Paper. This has just been published, in a handsome volume, at Lowestoft, by Samuel Tymms.

to have flourished about the beginning of the fourteenth century, and I fear we cannot put much faith in the *Symon*, as the "Norman thieves" were rather fond of the name.

Yarmouth, 2nd August, 1869.

I am greatly obliged to you for sending me full particulars of the history of the vessel fished up in a Suffolk stream in past days, and to Lady Pigot for the sketch of it. On further examination, I begin to grow dissatisfied with my own theory. The neck is narrowed, and the lower part of the bowl too much expanded for the mortars with which I am familiar. At the same time, the fact of its being made of bronze, with solid handles and feet of stoutness, would seem to indicate that it was intended for some purpose requiring unusual strength and durability; and as my York specimen is dated 1308, and Rabbi Sancto lived before that time, it may be the form of an older style of mortar. I will write to York for a photograph, and send you a copy, but the effect of it will not be to strengthen my case at all. I really do not know, however, why anything but English obstinacy should prevent my acknowledging that your theory is as likely to be correct as any other. I am beginning to quake upon another point—whether the vessel was cast at all, whether it was not rather the work of the smith than the founder. If the inscription were in high relief, it would make my mind comfortable again; but there is no way, I suppose, of eliciting this point. The reason for my doubting as to the vessel coming from a mould is the claw-like ending of the handles—they look so like riveting. I noticed the other day, at Hardwick, a bronze Etruscan jug with the lower end of the handle of something the same form, and loose, which would hardly be the case with a handle cast to the vessel; but at the upper end I could detect no trace of a joint. I managed to put a quiet question to Professor Churchill Babington about it; but he would not enter into the technology of the vessel. In the sketch which you kindly sent me, there is a distinct joint between the handles and the band which passes round the vessel connecting them. I dare not go further than express my suspicions as to the vessel ever having come from the mould.

Yarmouth, 6th October, 1869.

I put myself into communication with Mr. Fairless Barber a short time ago, on the subject of Yorkshire metallurgy; and the result has been a photograph of a vessel found at Wharncliffe, of the history of which he could tell me nothing. I enclose it for your acceptance, worthless as I fear it is. I must hunt up a certain Minor Canon of York, who was at Cambridge with me, and get a photograph of the York mortar for you; I am convinced that I am in the wrong about your vessel, and when I lecture on Bells, at Bury, at Christmas, all well, I will openly recant that my wicked error in canonical form.

APPENDIX.

APPENDIX.

A.—See page 13.

An eminent Cornish scholar of last century, who devoted a great deal of his time to prove the affinity between the Hebrew and the ancient Welsh languages, observed, "It would be difficult to adduce a single article or form of construction in the Hebrew grammar, but the same is to be found in Welsh, and that there were many whole sentences in both languages exactly the same in the very words." From two columns of quotations which that writer adduced I give the following as examples, and shall translate them according to their signification in the ancient Cornish:—

בני אלים:—Ps. xxix. 1.
Beni Elyv.
Reared ones of power.

מחיה מתים:
Mychweii Methion.
Thou dost quicken those that have failed.

בלע אדני את כל נאות יעקב:—Lam. ii. 2.
By-llwng adon-ydh holl neuodh Iago.
The Lord has swallowed up all the tabernacles of Jacob.

דרך ביתה יצעד:—Prov. vii. 8.
Dyrac buth hi ai-i-sengyd.
The avenue of her dwelling he would go to tread.

דרכי שאול ביתה יורדות אל חדרי מות:—Prov. vii. 27.
Dyracei sál buth-hi ea-warededh ill cadeirian méth.
That leads to vileness is her abode, going the descent to the seat of failing.

* בָּרוּךְ אַתָּה יְהֹוָה אֱלֹהֵינוּ מֶלֶךְ הָעוֹלָם:
Barwch wytti id el-eini maelog y-hwylma.

Seat of increase art Thou, Supreme, our intellectual Power, Possessor of the space of revolution.

Ps. vii. 11.—מָגִנִּי עַל אֱלֹהִים:
Meigen-i hwyl elyv.

My protection is from the intelligences.

Ps. xxiv. 10.—מִי הוּא זֶה מֶלֶךְ הַכָּבוֹד יְהֹוָה צְבָאוֹת הוּא מֶלֶךְ הַכָּבוֹד סֶלָה:

Py yw-o sy maeloc y-cavad I-A-YW-VO savwyod yw-o ma-elo_c y-cavad. Sela.

Who is He that is possessor of attainments? I THAT AM HIM of hosts, He is the possessor of attainments. BEHOLD.

Now, if the aboriginal Britons knew not the Jews, where could they have got hold of such whole Hebrew, purely Hebrew, sentences?

B.—See page 14.

וידעו כי שלח אנוסטוס קיסר בעצת אנטונינוס חברו בכל ארצות ממשלתו עד מעבר לים הודו ועד מעבר ארץ בריטאניאה והיא ארץ ים אוקיאנוס ויצו את כל מקום אשר בו איש או אשה מזרע היהודים עבד או אמה לשלחם חפשים בלא פדיון במצות הקיסר אנוסטוס ואנטונינוס חברו:

C.—See page 15.

הקיסר אנוסטי היה איש חסיד וירא אלהים והיה עושה משפט וצדקה ואוהב ישראל: ומה שכתוב בראש ספר שבט יהודה שקיסר אנוסטי עשה הרג רב ביהודים הלא המגיד כחש לו כי לא מצאתי רמז מזה בכל הקרוניקים שראיתי מימי: אדרבא בכל ספרי זכרונותיהם גם ביוסיפון פר' ט״ו כתב שהיה אוהב נאמן לישראל: גם בפר' מ״ז כתב שהקיסר הזה שלח כתב חרות ליהודים בכל ארצות ממשלתו למזרח עד מעבר לים הודו ולמערב עד מעבר ארץ בריטאניאה (היא מדינת אנגאלטירה הנקרא בל״א עננלאנד):

---

* The first sentence of almost all Jewish thanksgivings to this very day.

D.—See page 22.

Hollingshed relates the following episode:—

"The king being at Rhoan on a time, there came to him divers Jews, who inhabited that city, complaining that divers of that nation had renounced their Jewish religion, and were become Christians; wherefore they besought him that for a certain sum of money, which they offered to give, it might please him to constrain them to abjure Christianity, and to turn to the Jewish law again. He was content to satisfy their desires. And so receiving their money, called them before him, and what with threats, and putting them otherwise in fear, he compelled divers of them to forsake Christ, and to turn to their old errors. Hereupon the father of one Stephen, a Jew converted to the Christian faith, being sore troubled for that his son was turned a Christian, (and hearing what the king had done in like matters,) presented unto him sixty marks of silver, conditionally that he should enforce his son to return to his Jewish religion; whereupon the young man was brought before the king, unto whom the king said, 'Sirrah, thy father here complaineth that without his licence thou art become a Christian: if this be true, I command thee to return again to the religion of thy nation without any more ado.' To whom the young man answered, 'Your Grace, (as I guess,) doth but jest.' Wherewith the king being moved, said, 'What! thou dunghill knave, should I jest with thee? Get thee hence quickly and fulfil my commandment, or by St. Luke's face, I shall cause thine eyes to be plucked out of thine head.' The young man, nothing abashed thereat, with a constant voice answered, 'Truly I will not do it; but know for certain, that if you were a good Christian you would never have uttered any such words, for it is the part of a Christian to reduce them again to Christ which are departed from Him, and not to separate them from Him which are joined to Him by faith.'

"The king, herewith confounded, commanded the Jew to get him out of his sight. But the father perceiving that the king could not persuade his son to forsake the Christian faith, required to have his money again. To whom the king said, he had done so much as he promised to do, that was, to persuade him as far as he might. At length, when he would have had the king deal further in the matter, the king, to stop his mouth, tendered back to him half the money, and kept the other himself. All which increased the suspicion men had of his infidelity."

E.—See page 33.

Dr. Jost, in his "*Geschichte der Israeliten*," vol. vii., p. 119, in common with all anti-Christian Jews, (see Apropos Essay,) betrays all the venomous partiality which characterises the enemies of "truth and justice, religion and piety." That Jewish historian takes upon himself, without any reason whatever, to assert that "*den Anlass dazu gab ein getaufter Jude, ohne Zweifel durch seine Schuld, von seinen ehemaligen Genossen auf offener Strasse verfolgt wurde.*" "The occasion for it was afforded by a baptized Jew, who without doubt, [! ! !] through his own fault, was persecuted in the open street by his former co-religionists."

F.—See page 33.

The following three charters are of so remarkable a character, that I deem them to be worthy of re-production, in their original entirety.

(1.)

Rex omnibus fidelibus suis, et omnibus et Judæis et Anglis salutem. Sciatis nos concessisse, et prœsenti charta nostra confirmasse, Jacobo Judæo de Londiniis Presbytero Judæorum, Presbyteratum omnium Judæorum totius Angliæ. Habendum et tenendum quamdiu vixerit, libere, et quiete honorifice, et integre; ita quod nemo ei super hoc molestiam aliquam, aut gravamen inferre præsumat. Quare volumus et firmiter præcipimus, quod eidem Jacobo quoad vixerit, Presbyteratum Judæorum per totam Angliam, garantetis, manuteneatis, et pacifice defendatis. Et si quis ei super ea foris facere præsumpserit, id ei sine dilatione (salva nobis emenda nostra de forisfactura nostra) emendare faciatis, tanquam Dominico Judæo nostro, quem specialiter in servitio nostro retinuimus. Prohibemus etiam ne de aliquo ad se pertinente ponatur in placitum, nisi coram nobis, aut coram Capitali Justiciario nostro, sicut charta Regis Richardi fratris nostri testatur.

Teste S. Baethoniens, Episcopo, &c., Dat. per manum Huberti

Cantuariensis Archiepiscopi, Cancellarii nostri, apud Rothomagum 12 die Julii an. Reg. nostr. primo.

(2.)

Johannes Dei Gratia, &c. Omnibus fidelibus suis ad quos literæ præsentes pervenerint tam ultra mare quam citra. Mandans vobis et præcipiens, quatenus per quascunque villas et loca Jacobus Presbyter Judæorum, dilectus et familiaris noster transierit, ipsum salvo, et libere, cum omnibus ad ipsum pertinentibus, transire et conduci faciatis; nea ipsi aliquod impedimentum, molestiam, aut gravamen fieri sustineatis, plus quam nobis ipsis et si quis ei, in aliquo, forisfacere præsumpserit, id ei sine dilatione, emendari faciatis.

Teste Willelmo di Marisco, &c. Dat. per manum Hu. Cantuar. Archiep. Cancellarii nostri apud Rothomagum 31. die Julii anno Reg. nostr. primo.

(3.)

"Johannes Dei gratia, &c. Sciatis nos consessisse omnibus Judæis Angliæ et Normaniæ, libere et honorifice habere residentiam in terra nostra et omnia illa de nobis tenenda quæ tenuerunt de Rege Henrico, avo patris nostri; et omnia illa quæ modo rationabiliter tenent in terris et feodis, et vadiis et akatis suis: et quod habeant omnes libertates, et consuetudines suas, sicut eas habuerunt tempore prædicti regis H. avi patris nostri, melius et quietius et honorabilius. Et si querela orta fuerit inter Christanum et Judæúm, ille qui alium appelaverit ad querelam suam dirationandam, habeat Testes, scilicet legitimum Christianum et Judæum. Et si Judæus de querela sua breve habeurit, breve suum erit ei testis. Et si Christianus habeurit querelam adversus Judæum, sit Judicata per pares Judæi. Et cum Judæus obierit, non detineatur corpus suum super terram, sed habeat haeres suus pecuniam suam et debita sua, ita quod non inde disturbetur, si habeurit haeredem qui pro ipso respondeat, et rectum faciat de debitis suis et de forisfacto suo. Et liceat Judæis omnia quæ eis apportata fuerint, sine occasione accipere et emere, exceptis illis quæ de ecclesiæ sunt et panno sanguinolento. Et si Judæus ab aliquo appellatus fuerit sine teste, de illo appellatu erit quietus solo Sacramento suo super librum suum, et de appellatu illarum rerum quæ ad coronam nostram pertinent, similiter quietus erit solo Sacramento suo super Rotulum suum. Et si inter Christianum et Judæum fuerit dissentio de accomodatione alicujus pecuniæ, Judæus probabit catallum suum et Christianus lucrum. Et Liceat Judæs quiete vendere vadium, postquam certum erit, eum illud unum annum, et unum diem tenuisse. Et Judæi non intrabunt inplacitum, nisi eoram nobis, aut coram illis qui turres nostras custodierint, in quorum ballivis Judæi manserint. Et ubicunque Judæi fuerint, liceat eis ire ubicunque voluerint, cum omnibus catallis eorum, sicut res nostræ propriæ; et nulli liceat eas retinere, neque hoc eis prohibere. Et præcipimus quod ipsi quieti sint per totam Angliam et Normaniam de omnibus consuetudinibus et Theoloniis et modiatione vini sicut nostrum proprium catallum. Et mandamus vobis et præcipimus quod eos custodiatis, et defendatis, et manu teneatis, et prohibemus nequis contra chartam istam de hiis supredictis eos in placitum ponat super forisfacturam nostram; sicut charta Regi H. patris nostri rationabiliter testatur. Teste T. Humf. filio Petri Com. Essex. Willielmi de Meerscal. Com. de Pembr. Henr. de Bohun Com. de Hereford. Robert de Turnham, Willielmo Brywer, &c. Dat. per manum S. Well. Archidiac. apud Marleberg, decimo dei Aprilis Anno Regni nostri secundo. Charta 2 John, n 49.

The above gracious charter might well have been considered a fabrication, had the following one not been added soon.

Judæi Angliæ dant Domino Regi M. M. M. M. marc, pro Cartis suis conformandis, et missæ fuerunt Cartæ Gaufrido filio Petri et Stephano de Pertico, ut eas faciant legi eoram se, et eoram Dom. Londoniensi et Norwicensi Episcopis, et cum acceperit securitatem de illis quatuor mille marcis reddendis, tunc eis illas cartas eoram prædictis liberet—oblata 2 Fo. M. 3.

G.—See page 38.

This was the first royal interest taken in the conversion of the Jews. Individual cases of interest in the spiritual welfare of the house of Jacob were to be met with in earlier times than those of Henry III., even in John's time. In 1213, Richard, the then Prior of Bermondsey, built a house for the reception of Hebrew

Christians, which he called "The Hospital for Converts." A much earlier institution for the same purpose was founded at Oxford, and flourished for a considerable time.

Whilst scarcely a vestige of those institutions which were organised by private individuals can now be traced, the vestiges of the royal one stand out to the present day, in bold relief, and seem to demand examination as to the legitimacy of the transfer which has been inflicted upon the *Domus Conversorum*. A brief sketch of the vicissitudes of the institution up to the present time may not be altogether uninteresting.

The royal idea seemed to have found favour with some of the prelates of that period. Ten years after the idea was carried out, the then Bishop of Winchester endowed it with *one hundred pounds*, a considerable benefaction, as money was then valued. In the year 1248, a very rich Jew of London, Constantine Ahef by name, had the misfortune to be convicted of felony, whereby he forfeited all his houses, lands, tenements, &c., to the crown. The king bestowed the forfeitures upon his best establishment.

When Edward I. succeeded to the throne, he ordered that every Jew who made an avowal of THE FAITH, and possessed more property than he absolutely required for the maintenance of himself and family, should hand over the surplus to the fund of the House of Converts. The same king also made over to that institution all the fines to which the Jews might be subjected for the seven years following his accession. He also granted to the said "House" the poll-tax which was levied on the Israelites, and all deodands that might come to the crown from similar sources. The establishment was put on a more business-like footing. He remodelled the management thereof, and insisted upon proper accounts being kept of all the revenues belonging to the House, as well as of the outlays in its behalf. Those accounts were periodically to be rendered to the royal exchequer. Should a balance be realised, the same was to be applied towards the improvement of the fabric, and towards the promotion of further means for the service of God.

After the expulsion of the Jews, in 1290, the usefulness of the Institution gradually declined, and the fabric fell into comparative decay. A report to the same effect was made in 1310, which brought about a thorough repair of the house, the chapel, cloisters, and tenements, but it unfortunately also paved the way for the future misappropriation of the property, and the diverting it from the object of the charity, which the royal founder had in view. The Wardenship of the "Domus Conversorum" was annexed to the Mastership of the Rolls. It is true that when the conjunction of the functions took place, it was stated that no transfer of the revenues of the institution was contemplated, but rather "to secure the care and preservation of the House of Converts, with its edifices, chapel, enclosure, and recent buildings;" but the spoliation eventually followed for all that.

It is a fact well worthy of notice, that there were some Hebrew-Christians in this country between the periods of the banishment and return of the Jewish people. There is no consecutive chronicle of them during that period, but detached accounts are now and then met with which warrant the affirmation. For instance, in the thirtieth year of Edward III., we read of one John de Castell, who was admitted into the "Domus Conversorum" by the following writ:—"The king to his beloved chaplain, Henry de Ingleby, the guardian of our House of Converts, in our city, London, sends greeting. Because we wish that John of Castell—a convert from the Jewish religion, who lately came into our kingdom of England—may have such support in our said house, from our alms, as others of the same sort have had in the same house before his time. We command you to admit the same John into our house, and that you cause him to have from that house the prescribed allowance for one convert. The king being witness at Westminster, on the first of July." We also read of a Jew, William Pierce by name, who was converted to Christianity in the fifth year of Richard II., and had a daily allowance of twopence from the funds of the "Domus Conversorum." In the following reign of Henry IV., we road of a Jewess, Elizabeth, the daughter of a famous Rabbi Moses, who, having embraced Christianity, had a pension allowed her from that fund, of "one penny a day above the usual allowance." The endowment was recognised and made available as late as the year 1686, when two Hebrew Christians received pensions out of the property. It is somewhat suggestive, that notwithstanding that a goodly number of the house of Israel were added to the Church in this country during the eighteenth century, no instance is on record that claims were made on the endowment on the part of the Jewish believers. It shows that the members of the synagogue who had joined the Church were men of considerable wealth. It is also curious to find that in 1738 the royal exchequer granted out of the endowment, an annual allowance of five hundred pounds, for maintenance of "converts from Popery." The crowning achievement of misappropriation was effected in the first year of the reign of Her Most Gracious Majesty, when an Act of Parliament (1 Vict. c. 46) was passed, which converted the whole of the Hebrew-Christian estates into Crown property. It is a very puzzling act, and might afford ingenious Chancery lawyers a grand theatre for the exhibition of legal skill. The preamble of the bill states that the Rolls' estate was formerly "the site of the House or Hospital of Converts, or Converted Jews," and that the hereditaments thereto belonging had been granted by Edward III. to the Rolls' Office. The fact, however, is that Edward III. only assigned those estates to that office IN TRUST for carrying out the object of the endowments.

I never can pass through Fleet-street without casting a wistful glance towards the archway which leads to the chapel which originally belonged to the "Domus Conversorum." Very often indeed have I loitered about the sanctuary itself, with a yearning heart that it might be restored to its original object. It has still its ancient and strong walls of flint and cement, in the same style of building as the white tower of the Tower of London; an upper portion of it having fallen in ancient times, has been replaced by modern brickwork. This stands in the Rolls' Court, and the chapel is still in use for divine service, for the benefit of lawyers and others in the neighbourhood.

H.—See page 39.

Some thirty years ago a statement of the particulars contained in the preceding Appendix was drawn up and submitted to a London solicitor, but he gave his opinion that it was then too late to agitate the subject, as the Act of Parliament had settled it for ever. Recent repeals of Acts of Parliament by other Acts of Parliament would seem to lead one to believe that if it were too late then to agitate, it is not too late now. All honour is due to the Rev. W. Gray, the worthy Principal of the flourishing Domus Conversorum, Palestine Place, Bethnal Green, for having had the courage to initiate a new agitation. He has kindly permitted me to make use of the following reply which he received from Mr. J. S. Brewer, of the Public Record Office, to a letter which he had addressed to that gentleman on the subject:

[COPY.]

PUBLIC RECORD OFFICE,

24th May, 1869.

DEAR SIR,—The Rolls' Estate was originally given for the conversion of the Jews, as early as the reign of Edward I., but as the cause did not prosper, it was converted to its present purposes by Edward III. Even if it had not been so, all the property was given up to the Government in the life of the late Lord Langdale. And the Treasury now pay £5000 a year to the Master of the Rolls, with the allowance of £600 a year for a house, and £220 a year for the Rolls' Chapel, including the salaries of Reader, Preacher, and Organist, and all other expenses. I am afraid, therefore, that the hope of receiving the endowment to which you refer in your letter to me, is not very cheering. Your proper course would be to submit the case to the Lords of the Treasury.

Yours truly,

(*Signed*) J. S. BREWER.

With all due deference to Mr. Brewer's opinion, I should venture to suggest to the large body of Hebrew Christians in London, to petition, petition, petition, until even a Parliament which "feared not God nor regarded man" restored that property to its original purpose, spiritual and temporal.

I.—See page 40.

The Monkish historians tell us that it proved a case of such difficulty that the *postea* was thought proper to be returned to parliament. Parliament could not decide. Indeed, the strangeness of the accusation would have puzzled any body of men to decide. Four years were allowed to elapse before the charge was brought, and the principal witness was a little boy of about nine years of age, who stated that when he was about five years old he was playing in a certain street; the Jews allured him into the house of one Jacob, where they kept him a day and night, and then blindfolded him, and circumcised him. Yet strange to say, with his eyes blinded, and amidst the confusion of so painful an operation, the youthful boy was able to notice several minute particulars, which he narrated, but which certainly never had any existence, inasmuch as the particulars he related to have taken place after the circumcision have no connexion with that rite. In addition to the boy's unlikely story, there were no symptoms of any kind that witness had ever gone under such an operation. Under such circumstances, and with such unsatisfactory evidence, the poor Jews would doubtless have been honourably acquitted, but as this calumny originated, in all probability, with the ecclesiastics, they could not brook disappointment, and contrived therefore to become accusers, witnesses, and judges themselves.

The bishops accordingly insisted upon the matter being tried in their courts, and as soon as the charge was dismissed by parliament, as incapable of being proved satisfactorily, the professing ministers of Christianity, who stated that the boy was circumcised in derision and contumely of their Lord and Master, determined to take the law into their own hands. They maintained that such questions belonged exclusively to the jurisdiction of the church, and that the state had no right to interfere. Baptism and circumcision, they argued, being matters of faith, the ministers of that faith had, therefore, alone the right of deciding cases of that kind. The poor Jews were therefore once more dragged before a judge and jury, who were most inimical to them, whose avaricious affections were set on their hard-earned riches. One can easily guess the result of the judgment-seat, and the fate of the unfortunate Norwich Jews.

William Ralegh, Bishop of Norwich, acted as judge: the archdeacon and the priests as witnesses, who deposed on oath that they saw the boy immediately after he was circumcised, and that there were then all the signs that such an operation had been performed upon him. Why and wherefore the archdeacon and priests kept it so long, the judge did neither ask nor care. How it came to pass that the signs had, in the short space of four years, totally disappeared, the judge did not investigate. A certain Maude also deposed, in confirmation of the charge, that after the boy had been taken home, the Jews called upon her to warn her against giving him any swine's flesh to eat.—*The Jews in Great Britain*, pp. 231—4.

J.—See page 42.

Mr. Hudson Turner, in his "Domestic Architecture of the Middle Ages," and after him Mr. Samuel Tymms, gives the following account of Moyses' Hall:—

The police station, or Moyses' Hall, called also the "Jews' House," or the "Jews' Synagogue." A singular specimen of a dwelling-house of the end of the eleventh or beginning of the twelfth century, and one of the most interesting remains in the town.

In plan, the building is nearly square, measuring in round numbers about fifty feet either way. The ground floor is vaulted and divided into three alleys, by ranges of three arches of stone, springing from either round or square pillars, having Norman capital bases. The arch-ribs of the western alley are semicircular; in the others they are early pointed. The western division differs from the others, too, in being of greater width; the space between pillar and pillar being about sixteen feet, while in the others it is less than eleven feet. These differences in form and size, coupled with the fact that the western range has been in comparatively modern times dissevered from the others, and made to form part of the adjoining inn, have led some to suppose that they must have originally belonged to distinct though conjoined tenements; but this notion was satisfactorily set aside a few years since by the discovery of the original staircase to the upper floor, in the first arch between the western and middle alleys, with its perfect well, lighted by two small apertures, one pointed and the other square, and having a doorway into each alley. On the west side the vaulting was, within the memory of persons still living, eight feet deeper than at present, and the descent was by a small staircase from the present staircase. It appears originally to have had no windows on the ground floor.

On the upper, over the eastern vaultings, are two good transition Norman windows, each of two lights, square-headed and plain, under a round arch, with moulding and shafts in the jambs, having capitals of almost early English character. It is a good example of the external and internal details of windows of this date.

It will be observed that internally the masonry is not carried up all the way to the sill of the window; by this arrangement a bench of stone is formed on each side of it. The other part of the house has a perpendicular window, which may have replaced a Norman one.

The sculpture under this window, representing the wolf guarding the crowned head of St. Edmund, is worthy of notice. The upper part has been too much altered to enable us to make out exactly what it originally was; it may have been a tower, of which the upper part is destroyed, or it may have contained a doorway.

The fireplace is in the wall of partition on the first floor, and not towards the street, as in the Jews' house at Lincoln; but this fireplace is not part of the original work, though it probably replaced an older one. The principal entrance to the house would appear to have been on the east side. The present east wall is no part of the genuine building, but was erected in 1806. That tradition should have assigned the name of the "Jews' House" to this building, and also to the two tenements of the Norman period at Lincoln, is a fact not without significance, and worthy of attention. Being the wealthiest members of the community, it is not unlikely that the Jews constructed substantial habitations, as much for the security of their persons and property as from any other motive.

It is certain that in all early deeds relative to the transfer of tenements once held by Jews, those tenements are usually described as built of stone. It was not till the thirteenth century that the Israelites were subjected to that long-continued system of oppression and exaction which terminated in their expulsion from the country by Edward I., in the year 1290. That expulsion was accomplished in a manner so sudden and violent, that the memory of it was likely to be strongly impressed on the popular mind, and, indeed, to remain so impressed in any place where substantial monuments of their former residence still survived. This house is mentioned in the will of Andreus Scarbot, 1474, as the " ten. Auquet 'Regis, vocat'—Moyse Hall." It was the residence in 1514 of Richard Kyng, a benefactor to the town.

The Guildhall feoffees bought the hall about 1614, and converted it into a workhouse and house of correction. In 1721 it was a hospital or workhouse for thirty boys and girls, who were clothed in blue, faced with yellow ; but on the consolidation of the two parishes for the government of the poor, in 1740, the hospital was removed to the workhouse.

The building is now used as a police station. In 1858 it was repaired from designs by G. G. Scott, Esq., principally by subscription. The changes rendered necessary in the outside

APPENDIX.   79

repairs, have been carried out in a style more in harmony with
that of the ancient building ; the low-pitched gable having been
replaced by one of greater elevation, and the Italian turret which
crowned its summit, has given place to a plain square substantial one of oak, covered with shingles, and terminated by a vane
adopted from the former one.

Warton, in his "History of English Poetry," speaks of a
magnificent stone synagogue extant, at Bury St. Edmund's, in
his day.

K.—See page 47.

The then Marquis of Northampton, in the course of a letter to
Dr. Covell, dated "Castle Ashby, August 26, 1696," thus alludes
to the vessel :—" The Rabbinical porridge-pot is a great mystery.
I can conceive it nothing but what is carried about in the
synagogues in imitation of the pot of manna,* whose form is not
very different from the description of this, as may be seen on the
shekel, one of which, if I remember, you have by you, and
several are exhibited in Walton's Prolog. to the Polyglott. I
guess this because—" [Here follows a maudlin attempt to explain
the transcript of the inscription, which neither the copyist nor the
marquis could read. The latter then proceeds,] "To me the
whole result of this groping in the dark seems to be this, that
the dedicator had made a visit to the Holy City, (the merit of
which is as much amongst them [the Jews] as the Papists to
Loretto, or the Mahommedans to Mecca,) and upon his return dedicated this vessel to his church. How far I am from the mark

---

* The above item of information will astonish the Jews ; it will be so new
to them, like many other Gentile interpretations of Jewish customs and
manners.

I can't tell; but this is all the light I can gain, at this distance, from the thing itself," &c., &c.

The following is an extract from Isaac Abendana's letter to Dr. Covell, dated " Oxon, October 9th, 1696:"—"As to the picture of the pot, it is a hard matter to conjecture with any certainty without some farther circumstances that may clear it. First, whether there was anything in when found? Whether it had any cover? The name of the place where it was found? If you can satisfy me thereof, may be will conduce much toward the finding out something. In the meantime I have set down as I can. I do not know of any vessel that is used at present in our synagogue but these: a vessel for the priests, or of the seed of Aaron, to wash their hands, when they go to bless the people; secondly, a vessel to go about the synagogue to collect alms. There is sometimes made such a vessel to preserve the ashes of some eminent man that died a martyr for his religion, and so it is difficult to know for which of these uses it was intended. I leave you to conjecture the most probable of the two last," &c., &c. [Here follows a poor attempt at an analysis of a *nondescript* inscription.]

L.—See page 51.

The Latin interpretation of the inscription, by Mr. Gagnier:—

Votum.

Josephi filii τοῦμακαρίτου Rabbi Jechielis,
Memoria Justi τοῦμακαρίτου fit in Benedictionem,
Qui reddit id, quod commodato acceperat,*
Synagogæ ¹Kahwelensi;
Quatenus mereatur videre faciem ²Arielis,
In cœtu,† in Lege ³Jekutielis;
Et Justitia liberabit à Morte.

¹*Kahwel*, nomen urbis Provinciæ Volhyniæ, in Poloniæ.‡
²*Ariel*, i.e., *Leo Dei*, nomen Altaris Templi Hierosolymitani.
³*Jekutiel*, i.e., *Expectatio Dei*, sic appelatur populus Judaiicus adventum Messiæ, de quo in precibus suis quotidie dicunt: *Veniat cito in diebus nostris.* §

M.—See page 56.

The following brief account of De Lyra is given by Bishop Bale in his "Illustrium Majoris Brittaniæ Catalogus."

Nicolaus Lyranus ex Judæorum genere Anglus; atque Hebræorum Rabbinos in literis Hebraicis ab ipsa pueritia

---

* Ignorance of the technical phrase for Rabbinical expositions and disquisitions dictated the above translation.

† The interpreter had here mistaken the grouping of the letters; instead of reading, as he ought to have done, בכתב דת, he read בכת בדת, hence the eccentric translation.

‡ This is an ingenious invention, in the absence of a better knowledge of the Hebrew language; else the otherwise learned Frenchman would have translated the word כהואל, according to its import.

§ Nor was Mr. Gagnier more successful here; the information respecting the Jews calling the coming of the Messiah Jekutiel, is by no means reliable.

nutritus, illud idioma sanctum ad unguem, ut loquuntur, novit. Qui mox ut frequentasset scholas publicas, ac minoritarum quorundam sincerioris judicii audisset conciones; abhorrere cœpit a Talmudicis doctrinis, atque ita a tota sua gentis insania stultissima. Conversus ergo ad Christi fidem, ac regenerationis lavacro lotus, Franciscanorum familiæ, se statim adjunxit. Inter quos scripturis sanctis studiosissimus ac longa exercitatione peritus, Oxonii et Parisiis, cum insulsissimis Rabbinis, qui plebem Judaicum vana Messiæ adventuri pollicitatione lactaverant disputationibus et scriptis, mirifice conflictavit. Denique contra eorum apertissimas blasphemias, utrumque Dei testamentum diligentiori examine et elucidatione explanavit. Si in plerisque, ut ei a multis imponitur, deliravit, tempori est imputandum, in quo fere omnia erant hypocritarum nebulis obscurata. Meliorem certe cæteris omnibus per eam ætatem navavit in scripturis operam. De verborum simplicitate non est quod conqueritentur homines, cum a vocabulis æstimanda non sit æterni patris veritas. Præclara scripsit opuscula, ut prædictus Tritemius habet, quibus nomen suum celebriter devenit ad posteritatis notitiam. Doctor Martinus Lutherus, in secundo et nono capitibus in Genesim, se ideo dicit amavisse Lyranum atque inter optimos posuisse quod præ cæteris interpretibus diligente fuerit historiam prosecutus. Claruit A.C. 1337, quo Danielem exposuit, ac Parisiis demum obiisse fertur.

AN APROPOS ESSAY.

7

AN APROPOS ESSAY.

WHATEVER opinion the intelligent reader may have formed touching the manner in which the subject, in the preceding pages, has been treated; he must have come to one conclusion only respecting the matter, which has been brought in bold relief, under consideration in those pages. Every sober, serious, thoughtful reader must admit that the subject matter is prolific of manifold suggestions. It suggests an indissoluble connexion between sacred and secular history; especially as regards the chronicles of the nation and people of Israel. It suggests that the best and shortest method by which to put to silence shallow-minded sceptics, would-be philosophical free-thinkers—the so-called rationalistic neologians of the present day—is to recommend the modern disciples of Spinoza, or Voltaire, a more critical study of the annals of Israel—ancient and modern—than their masters, just named had ever enjoyed.* It suggests that Israel is a sort of KOSMOS, that the history of the nation is as peculiar as the people themselves. PECULIAR in the Bible sense, and in the modern secular sense. It suggests that in whatever country the scattered seed of Israel had been sown—I use advisedly a prophetic idiom †—there it not only took deep root, but when it sprang up into a tree, with wide spreading branches, the latter became so entwined with the branches of the native trees, that to describe the growth of the one without that of the other, would prove an imperfect, and therefore unreliable description. It suggests the truth—and the applicability of it to all times—of the great apostolic dictum, " Even so, then, at this present time, there is a remnant according to the election of grace." ‡ The Jewish people—bitter and intolerant as their national hostility has hitherto been to the terms of the NEW TESTAMENT,

---

* The most erudite, philosophical, and masterly exposure of Voltaire's attacks—in his Philosophical Dictionary and other works—upon the Hebrew Scriptures and nation, has been published, just a century ago, under the title of "Letters de quelques Juifs, Portuguais, Allemandes, et Polonais." The work has gone through many editions, in the original, since it was first published. In England, or rather in Ireland, a very indifferent translation of it appeared soon after the first original edition was published, and has been out of print a few years short of a hundred. A new translation of the last French edition, edited with ability, so as to embrace the sceptical lucubrations of recent years, would prove a most valuable defence of THE FAITH, at this present day. I am glad to say that Lady Pigot has courageously undertaken the task of TRANSLATOR and EDITOR.

† Hosea ii. 23.   ‡ Rom. xi. 5.

or COVENANT—have never been without some of "the Israel of God."* In the darkest and gloomiest hours of the Christian Church at Rome, there was a Saul, or Paul, who could boldly stand up and triumphantly ask, "I say, then, Hath God cast away His people?" Answer, "God forbid! For I also am an Israelite, of the seed of Abraham," &c., &c.,† *i.e.*, "I am a living and moving argument against the preposterous supposition."

I might contrive to gather in a very large harvest of suggestions, for the fecundity of the subject matter is in this respect almost illimitable, but let every reader be his own reaper. There is only one suggestion more that I wish to name, as the starting-point of this little Essay; namely, that the annals of the Anglo-Hebrews provide as fine a field for a Niebuhr as the History of Rome ever proved. The Tower, the Chapter-House, Westminster Abbey, the Public Record Office, &c., &c., ‡ abound with materials for such a literary enterprize. But a stubborn question arises. "What class of Her Majesty's subjects, in this country, can present so candid, impartial, and critical a Niebuhr—at once so equal to the task, and disposed to do justice to every portion of the Jewish nation in this country? The Gentiles, or the Jews themselves?" It may be answered by the former :—

* See Note * p. 22.
† Rom. xi. 1.
‡ Mr. J. Burtt, of the Public Record Office, is now engaged upon a catalogue, for the printer, of the ancient deeds in all the above-named archives; he assures me that the Hebrew Shĕtars are both numerous and interesting.

"Of course we have the men equal to the task. Look at our Stanley, our Froude; they are only representatives of large classes, of our able historians, in Church and State." I reply,

"Neither your Stanley nor your Froude—fair representatives though they be of large classes of your able historians in Church and State—possess the peculiarly requisite qualification for writing the history of the dispersed of Israel, since the dismemberment of the nation. To write such a history, it is necessary to be conversant with the whole range of Hebrew literature, since the close of the canon of Scripture. Very often a single sentence only, may be detected in a scarce Hebrew volume, which gives the clue to the solving of a perplexing historical problem. Such an acquaintance neither a Gentile Stanley, nor a Gentile Froude possess."

"Not a Stanley! Did he not publish a sparkling 'History of the Jewish Church!'"

"Yes, yes; that was the Jewish Church of the Old Testament. His materials for it were made ready to his hand, in the existing translations of the Hebrew Scriptures, as well as other auxiliaries, such as Ewald's productions, &c. Even with all those accessories, he fell into many grave errors, by reason of not possessing a critical knowledge of the original. A specimen error I pointed out in a note to an article which I wrote for the 'Scattered Nation,' for January 1866."

"Cannot the Anglo-Hebrews themselves, who, undoubtedly, have many learned men amongst them, produce a historian equal to the task of writing the annals of the Jews in this country ? "

Hitherto, whilst the English Jews have distinguished themselves in various literary and scientific pursuits, they have not attempted a history of their people in this country. I cannot conceal my conviction that a Niebuhr-Jewish historian cannot be found in any of the synagogues of Europe. The Jewish people of the present day may be thus classified, (1) Talmudical, (2) " Reformed," and (3) Christian. The antipathy which exists between the two former, towards one another, is almost as virulent as that between Ultramontane Roman Catholics and Hibernian Orangemen. They cannot speak of one another with impartiality, much less write so. They brand each other with the most disparaging stigmas. Such persons as are in the habit of reading the Jewish newspapers and periodicals, published at home and abroad, will endorse the truth of my statement. Let me be thoroughly understood, 1 am speaking of the writing members of those two sections. There are many noble exceptions, in either body, to specimens of which I shall presently allude ; but those exceptions— for reasons that I shall anon make plain—do not trouble themselves about controversial subjects, or Jewish history.

Whilst the former two sections of the " House of Israel " are at constant feuds amongst themselves, they invariably coalesce in vilifying the last-named, and smaller, section of their people, namely, the Christian Jews. Implacable virulence, and deadly hate, marks the attitude of the two former towards the latter. Their organs in this country, as well as on the continent, breathe uncharitable denunciations against the "remnant according to the election of grace." Yet a historian of the annals of the Jewish nation would have to notice the existence of that remnant—it is on the increase every day! Would either the Talmudical Jew, or the "Reformed" Jew, treat them with candour and justice? Certainly not. Let any one peruse the Jewish Weeklies in this country, and he will see the gratuitous and frenzied obloquy heaped, by their penmen, upon the Christian Jews; those the scribblers repeat, unabashed, over and over again, after the falsehood of their statements has been exposed a hundred times. Just like so many Codruses and Welsteds, whom Pope, the prince of English satirists, appropriately described in the following lines:—

> "Who shames the scribbler? Break one cobweb through,
> He spins the slight, self-pleasing thread anew;
> Destroy his fib or sophistry; in vain,—
> The creature's at his dirty work again.
> * * * * *
> Full ten years slandered—did I e'er reply?
> Three thousand suns went down, on Welsted's lie!"

"The remnant according to the election of grace," may change the first three words of the last-quoted couplet into "Full eighteen hundred years." Such has been the experience of "the remnant," from the nation's Scribes, Pharisees, Sadducees, and Priests, ever since the Redeemer began to call sinners to repentance. Many a time did the fourfold hostile element of unbelief coalesce to crush out THE FAITH from the midst of the nation; but THE FAITH has been leavening the nation—now more, now less—ever since it was promulgated, and never more so than at this present time. The above-named coalition was never more rampant, more fierce, more reckless in their libellous statements against "the remnant," than since the beginning of this century. The historians which either the Talmudical, or the "Reformed" Jews have since produced have proved themselves partial, narrow-minded, unscrupulous, unjust, and unreliable, when they spoke or wrote of Christian Jews.* It will be long ere the virulent attack is forgotten, which the Jews of London made upon Mr. Samuda, at the late general election; simply because he dared to be obedient to the dictates of his conviction and conscience, and own the divine claims of Israel's New Testament as well as the Old. Well might a Gentile Christian have exclaimed, "Ah! what a fate for Christians, if such Israelites as scribble in the Jewish papers swayed the sceptre of political authority!"

I have named this Essay APROPOS, for more reasons than one; the most apparent one will be found in the several digressions, which occurred to my mind, as I was carried along in the train of thought on the main subject, but I considered them at the same time *apropos* to the grand junction. There is an episode in the life of the late Dr. M'Caul, the most faithful and true Gentile-Christian-friend that the Jewish nation has

* As a specimen, see Appendix F.

ever had, which seems to me to be relevant to the topic under review.

Whilst Dr. M'Caul resided at Warsaw, a very learned chief rabbi, upwards of fifty years of age, from a neighbouring town, called upon him, and solicited further instruction in the Christian religion; as he was convinced that Judaism without Christianity was only "the shadow of death." On entering into conversation with the enquirer, Dr. M'Caul found him a man of great learning, having a soul deeply solemnized, a spirit profoundly devout, and a heart breaking to be at peace with God. No Gentile knew the Jews better than Dr. M'Caul did, he therefore said to his visitor:—

"My good rabbi, you know the animosity which your people evince towards one of themselves who returns to the teaching of the Bible, with regard to their Redeemer. You know that they will not scruple to accuse you of the most heinous crimes, and inconsistencies, the moment that they find out that you are feeling your way back again to the fold of Israel's Shepherd."

"Yes," rejoined the sorrow-stricken rabbi, "I thought of that too. I know that, though to-day I am esteemed by my people as one of the saints of the earth, to-morrow—when the step which I am determined to take shall transpire—my name shall be cast out as evil, and all manner of false accusation will be hurled against me. I have, however, provided against THE FAITH being sullied on my account. Here is the means of rebutting any attempt against my character. I told my people that I was about to resign my post, and remove to Warsaw. As I was a stranger in the Polish metropolis, I asked the heads of the congregation to testify to my religious and moral character, according as they conscientiously thought of me. Read what they say, and keep the paper by you."

Dr. M'Caul read the testimonial, numerously and influentially signed; it endorsed the high opinion which he had formed of his visitor, and Rabbi Abraham Jacob Schwartzenberg became one of his catechumens, preparatory to receiving the sacrament of baptism. When the leading men, of the rabbi's ex-congregation, heard thereof, they came to Warsaw, sought out Dr. M'Caul, and overwhelmed him with hideous charges of dishonesty, immorality, and impiety, against their former pastor. To whom the Christian minister quietly rejoined, "Possibly Rabbi Abraham Jacob Schwartzenberg is as disreputable as ye represent him to be; but in what repute do ye hold the men who signed THIS TESTIMONIAL!" He suited the action to the word, and held up the instrument before the eyes of the accusers, that they might see their own names. Of course they left the house covered with shame and confusion of face. But did the slanderers cease their revilings? No; they circulated a report that their late rabbi had gone mad.

One word more about Schwartzenberg. He lived for upwards of twenty years after his admission into the Church by baptism; he never laid aside his long national dress, he mixed amongst his brethren, notwithstanding their cruel ill-treatment, and lovingly preached the Gospel to them. The Jews labour under a sort of hallucination, that every Hebrew-Christian, on his death-bed, recants his Christian profession of faith, by repeating the words, "Hear, O Israel, the LORD our God is one LORD;" the Jews of Warsaw were therefore on the *qui vive* when the vital spark in that venerable "Israelite indeed" was about to quit the mortal frame. They crowded the dying saint's chamber. What were his very last words on earth to be?— "Brethren, you wish to know in what faith I am dying! If every drop of blood in me were vocal, endowed with speech, each such drop would cry aloud that I am dying full of joy and peace, believing in the redemption of Israel, through the Lord Jesus Christ." He spoke no more on earth after that.*

> "Blush, Calumny! and write on his tomb,
> If honest eulogy can spare thee room,
> Thy deep repentance!"

The Jewish Codruses and Welsteds are very fond of telling their readers what certain "Christians" think of "the remnant." Let me put them in possession of the view of "the remnant" touching this part of the story. As for the opinion which the spiritually ignorant, *i.e.*, the mere nominal Gentile "Christian," forms of the Hebrew Christians, picked up from some antichristian Jew, it is to the maligned a matter of perfect indifference. Those "Christians" can as much under-

* A portrait of that Christian Israelite appears as a frontispiece to the first edition of my "Fundamental Principles of Modern Judaism Investigated."

stand the soul's conversion, as the born blind can comprehend the beauty of the colours of the rainbow, or as the born deaf can appreciate the melody and harmony of the "Creation," or as the poor demented maniac can understand the connexion between the subject and predicate of a logical syllogism. Those "Christians" are probably altogether ignorant that

> "'Twas a Jew that shed His blood
> Our pardon to procure;
> 'Tis a Jew that sits above,
> Our blessings to secure."

The fact would probably be new to those "Christians" that Hebrew Christians were moved by the Spirit of God to pen the sublime records contained in the New Testament. Such "Christians" may well sit at the feet of anti-christian Jews, and learn of them how to revile "the Israel of God."

Those Jewish masters, along with their Gentile disciples, affect to sneer at Hebrew Christians, because the latter have renounced the religion—which was invented by the Talmudists, and withal so repugnant to sound reason, revelation, and common sense—in which they were born.* It is a pet, though a very silly, phrase, with such sapient philosophers, that a man ought to die in the religion in which he was born, be it ever so untenable; and that, notwithstanding that

* I am revising and enlarging the last edition of my "Fundamental Principles of Modern Judaism Investigated." It will appear under the more comprehensive title, "The Whole Plan of Post-Biblical Judaism."

revelation has made known ONLY ONE, "Holy, Just, and Good!" Were the aboriginal Britons wrong in having given up their hideous and murderous form of idolatry for " the glorious Gospel of the living God ?" In what condition would now the British sages have been, if all their ancestors had died worshippers of Odin, or Thor? Were Copernicus and Galileo wrong in accepting a different creed, with respect to the solar system, from that in which they were born, bred, and educated? No, no; principles are not necessarily sound, simply because our forefathers espoused them; nor are creeds inevitably tenable, or orthodox, because they were instilled into our minds from our cradles.

The goodwill which the Hebrew Christians value they possess. The spiritually-educated Gentile Christians know full well that the former were the founders of the Christian Church. They are well aware that the "Israel of God" are, at the present moment, most important witnesses for God's truth in the midst of a perverse and gainsaying generation, and they treat them accordingly. Let me just adduce an illustration. Last year was held a very influential meeting of the clergy of the deanery of East Chester, at Gateshead, under the presidency of the Archdeacon of Durham. There were about thirty clergymen present; the subject for consideration was the "Convocation of the two Provinces." Who was selected to draw up a paper on the important question? We were informed through the public press, metropolitan and provincial, that the Rev. Samuel Asher Herbert,

Rector of St. James's, Gateshead, " read an able and interesting paper upon the defects in the constitution of Convocation of the Church." The paper was unanimously adopted by the meeting of learned and Christian gentlemen; and those who have read the *Brochure* must pronounce it a masterpiece.* Who is the Rector of St. James's, Gateshead? An Anglo-Hebrew Christian—grandson of the founder of the Bedford synagogue. He was introduced into the Christian Church, by the sacred ordinance of baptism, in 1836, at the ripe age of twenty-three; the officiating minister being the catechumen's uncle, himself a former rabbi of Bedford. Upwards of twenty persons from that single family are now consistent members of the Christian Church.

A worthy relative of mine, at Paris, has published this year a clever work, entitled " Eighteen Centuries of Christian Prejudice,"† being an appeal on the part of the Jews to the Gentiles, against the long and deep-rooted hatred which the latter entertain towards the former; as well as a protest against the unjust calumnies with which the Gentiles aspersed the Jews during those long eighteen hundred years. *Mutatis mutandis*, it would be an apposite title for an appeal, on the part of " the remnant," to the residuary of the Jewish nation, on the same score which my Jewish kinsman pleads with Gentile Christians.

* " *Convocation:* Its present constitution, and its requirements for the work of the Church."

† "Dix-huit Siècles de Préjugés Chrétiens," Par Léon Hollændersky.

Let me now, after this long, though apropos digression, return to the principal topic of the Essay. Every well-informed scholar must maintain that neither the representatives of the Talmudical, nor those of the " Reformed " Jews, are qualified to write an unprejudiced history of the Anglo-Hebrews, or of the Hebrew nation anywhere. I would go a step farther, and maintain that the eighteen centuries of prejudice has disqualified the representatives of the residuary—I mean the Christ-rejecting Jews,—to write soberly, critically, with a " literary conscience," on any subject which appertains, directly or indirectly, to their system of theology. As an illustration, I need only mention the notoriously highly-coloured and romantic article, which appeared a couple of years ago in the " Quarterly Review," under the title *Talmud*. I dare say, I may be reminded of one of Seneca's old " saws," "Gallus in suo sterquilinio plurimum potest." But I venture to affirm that no bantam has ever had the assurance to make such a jubilant noise, over so unsavoury a heap—notwithstanding the few-and-far-between grains which may be scratched out of it—as some Jews have made over the Talmud since that article was published. The marvel is, that many sceptical Gentile "Christians" should take the writer's *ipse dixit* for sober truth.

"Then where is the Niebuhr for an ANGLO-HEBREW HISTORY to be found?" I answer, fearlessly, amongst Anglo-Hebrew Christians. The majority of those men have passed through a discipline which fits them for the critical examination of the most complex questions. They were born and bred in a system which they were led to hold as utterly incontrovertible ; by a process of most scrutinising enquiry, and searching examination of evidence *pro* and *con*, they have at last arrived at the conviction that the Judaism which they had hitherto professed, was not only defective, or incomplete, but also fearfully corrupt. So strong was their conviction, that they braved the greatest losses that a Jew can possibly experience, even the severance of the nearest and tenderest ties. Nothing short of the most irrefragable and overwhelming evidence could have induced them to become obedient to THE FAITH in the covenant completed on Calvary. The structure of the Hebrew Christian's mind is such as to refuse to take in any theory, or statement, on trust; it must weigh everything in the justest balances; it must try every thought in the most refining crucible. The Hebrew Christians are, moreover, jealous of their nation's honour ; they take every opportunity to point out that which is great, good, and noble amongst the members of the Jewish community. Though the latter revile, the former bless ; the latter persecute, the former bear patiently ; the latter defame, the former live down.

" But we are constantly assured, by the Jews themselves, that only the poorest and most ignorant of their nation change their religion, and that from sordid motives." There can be no doubt that there are some poor and ignorant Jews in the Christian Church, as well as in the Jewish synagogue, and possibly, now and then, an unprincipled Jew, as well as an unprincipled Gentile, trades upon religion; but such are rare instances indeed amongst Hebrew Christians. Though Christianity does not profess to improve a poor man's temporal prospects, it professes, and carries the profession into effect, to improve the ignorant and wicked man's mental and moral character. The young woman, Esther Lyons, whose case attracted lately so much attention, is now a far better educated person than she was whilst in her unhappy home, at Cardiff. Such cases, however, as I have said, are but very seldom to be met with amongst Hebrew Christians. Their Jewish enemies try to persuade you, Gentile Christians, that the rare exception is the rule. Be on your guard; take not the communications of your informants, on that subject, as emanations from oracles of truth. The enlightened, better educated, and liberal-minded Jews do not treat those calumniators as oracles of truth—they feel an irresistible shrinking from the touch of such bigots, though they, now and then, hold out a reluctant hand to the slanderers. The enlightened, well informed Jew is no bigot, no railer, no false accuser. There are noble and impartial spirits amongst the Jews everywhere, who, with praiseworthy liberality, do justice to such of their brethren as have seen reason to recognise the Divine authority of the New Testament.

I will illustrate this, my statement, by a couple of quotations from Jewish works of this present century.

The late Rabbi Isaac Beer Levinsohn, of Kremnitz, in Russia, in his well-written Hebrew work

אפס דמים, *Ephes Damim*, purporting to be a series of conversations, at Jerusalem, between a patriarch of the Greek Church, Simmias by name, and a chief rabbi of the Jews, Abraham Maimonides by name, concerning the foul charge against the Jews, of using Christian blood, which was then revived. Rabbi I. B. Levinsohn puts the following candid confession into the mouth of Maimonides:—

רוב המומרים היום מאצילי בני ישראל ועל פי
רוב מלומדים בלשונות שונות ובחכמות או עשירים
מופלנים . . . . ובקושי ימצא היום מומר
מהזכרים שיהיה איש בור וריק:

"The majority of converts now-a-day are from the nobles of the children of Israel; and are generally learned in various languages and sciences, or wonderfully wealthy . . . . . . And with difficulty can now-a-day a convert be found, who is either unlearned, or uninformed."

That northern rabbi's sentiment found an echo in the mind of a rabbi in the east, in the very place where anti-christian Jews were so fearfully branded, at Smyrna. (Rev. ii. 8—10.) I happened to be, in 1848, in "the queen of the cities of Anatolia"—known in the days of yore as "the crown of Ionia," "the ornament of Asia." I found the Jews numerous there, learned, and generally well-to-do. I paid a visit to their chief, and really great, Rabbi Chayim Palagi. That master in Israel received me cordially. In the course of a long interview, we conversed on various subjects touching the state of parties, and their respective conditions, amongst the Jews in Europe. I particularly dwelt on the three classes into which the Anglo-Hebrews are ranged, Talmudical, "Reformed," and Christian. I asked the venerable man whether he had heard of the interest which the Anglo-Hebrew Christians took in the sufferings of their anti-christian brethren at Damascus, when the latter were accused, a few years ago, of murdering a Roman Catholic priest, in order to secure his blood for the Passover festival? The question put the rabbi in the very best of humours, for he had an opportunity of referring to a work of his, which he had published on the subject, in the shape of a sermon. He spoke in the same breath of Sir Moses Montefiore, and of Mr. Pieritz—now Rector of Hardwicke, diocese of Ely— the Anglo-Hebrew Christian who personally pleaded the cause of the persecuted Jews before the pacha. The rabbi owned that the latter did more than the former for the exculpation of the Hebrews from the foul calumny. He went up to one of his book-shelves, and took down a volume—it was his published sermon, which he dedicated to Sir Moses Montefiore—and read out the following passage:—

וגם כמה מהחכמים שלנו שהמירו דתם האם
יכול אחד מהם להאמין בדבר הזה וכו׳:

"And even the many of our wise men who have changed their religion, does any one of them believe in this thing?" &c., &c.

"This will convince you," said R. Chayim Palagi to me, "that I have great respect for Jewish Christians.

I do not deny that many wise and many learned are to be found amongst them. May I ask you to accept this volume, as a memento of sincere friendship on my part ?" Of course I accepted the book.*

The late Sir J. L. Goldsmid, a Jewish baronet, when addressing a meeting, on the 28th of May, 1844, respecting the Jewish Literary and Scientific Institution, said, " I will just mention a fact which has just come to my knowledge, that out of the one hundred and forty-two professors in the Berlin University, fourteen of them are Jews, certainly converted ones, but still Jews." The candid Jew everywhere acknowledges that the change of sentiment, for the better, amongst Gentile Christians, towards the Jewish community, is owing, in a great measure, to the pleadings of Hebrew Christians in its behalf.

Such exceptional Israelites as the three examples which I have just adduced, are neither scarce nor uncommon. Unfortunately, however, those enlightened and liberal-minded Jews do not care to become historians of their nation. There are many things in the annals of the people of which free thinking Jews—I use the term not in an opprobrious sense—have reason to be ashamed. They know, moreover, the enormous capacity for abuse which bigotry possesses and employs. Not having gone through the school and discipline of most Hebrew Christians, they have not the courage of the latter. They feel somewhat like the late Duke of Wellington, when he said to Rogers, " I

* " A Pilgrimage to the Land of my Fathers." Vol. II., pp. 159, 160.

should like to tell the truth, but if I did, I should be torn to pieces, here or abroad." Indeed there are many highly respectable Jewish families, in this country, who have joined the Church, and keep the fact an inviolable secret. The Nicodemus type of Hebrew Christians was at all times to be found amongst the Jewish people.

At the close of the year 1862, when I resided in Huntingdon, I was invited to London to baptize privately a whole Sephardim family, consisting of twenty-two members—aged father and mother, six sons, three daughters, four daughters-in-law, and seven grandchildren. The interesting catechumens particularly stipulated that the sacrament should be administered to them under the seal of secrecy, as they had an irresistible antipathy to publicity. As a clergyman of the Church of England, I could not minister in another man's parish without the permission of "the powers that be." I was obliged, therefore, to put myself into communication, on the subject, with the then Bishop of London— the present Archbishop of Canterbury—and the Rev. H. Howarth, Rector of St. George's, Hanover Square. To both those authorities I have made known all the particulars of that most interesting case. My communications to them were, respectively, dated November 24th, 27th, and December 1st, 1862.

There are certain impertinent persons amongst the anti-christian Jews, who have the assurance to ask for the publication of the names of the Hebrew Christians in England! What for? That they might indulge in coarse abuse against some of the best men, and most consistent Christians, when a parliamentary election shall again take place. To vilify other Hebrew Christian candidates as they have maligned Mr. Samuda ! ! !

There are, however, many eminent Hebrew Christians, whose moral prowess is invincible. "Truth against the world," though only recently adopted by the Laureate, has been their motto for upwards of eighteen hundred years. A reliable, sound, critical, and unbiassed history of the Jews, either in this land or in other lands, can only be got from the pens of the learned amongst the " Israelites indeed." A college for such men—not the bantling of a society— a chartered college, under the government and chancellorship of distinguished Anglo-Hebrew Christians, might prove the nursery of the purest literature and soundest science.

" How do I propose to raise the money for the required fabric and endowment?" By Act of Parliament! Repeal the Spoliation Act of Anno Primo Victoriæ Reginæ, cap. XLVI. Let the vast accumulated property of the " Domus Conversorum," in Chancery Lane, and Fetter Lane, be restored to its proper object; and a well-endowed college—with its chapel, and residences for professors, students, porters—is ready to hand. The new Public Record Office would not be a bad college to begin with. Why not add " Sion College " to it ?

When the Hebrew Christian, Sir Francis Palgrave, was appointed Master of the Rolls, some facetious humourist, at the time, put a question in the "Notes and Queries," to the effect, "How long since was it that the property of the 'Domus Conversorum' had been restored to its original purpose?" When I read it, I could not help observing, "Many a true word spoken in jest." Some may probably be disposed to treat this, my proposition, as a jest. Let me assure my readers that I am thoroughly and soberly in earnest.

Is there no cause for courageous earnestness in the matter! Nay, has not the time arrived for Anglo-Hebrew Christians to be the most outspoken, of all her Majesty's subjects, in this land! There is no department in the realm—whether it be political, ecclesiastical, civil, literary, or commercial—which some Hebrew Christians do not adorn. The "Israelites indeed" have their representatives in the Senate, at the Bar, in the Church, on the Exchange, and in the Mart. The arts and the sciences count the children of "the remnant" amongst their most genuine supporters. Thank God, the Anglo-Hebrew Christians are ornaments to every profession, quality, or trade with which their names happen to be associated.

Printed at the Operative Jewish Converts' Institution, Palestine Place, Bethnal Green, E.

Works Published by the same Author.

I.
ABYSSINIA: ITS PAST, PRESENT, AND PROBABLE FUTURE.
A Lecture, with Notes and Appendices. Published by Request. Price 3s.

"We felt whilst reading it that it is the production of a man thoroughly acquainted with the subject: of one who enters into it fully equipped with all that is required to do it justice, for he possesses Biblical, geographical, and historical knowledge. The book reads like a romance, and has all the charms which a loving heart alone can impart even to the writing of truth."—*The Scattered Nation.*

"Besides the direct object of the lecture, the writer has treated on several important Biblical matters, in the preface, notes, &c."—*The Clerical Journal.*

"Dr. Margoliouth has stated the case against the Foreign Office very clearly, and it is impossible not to admit the force of his reasoning."—*The Athenæum.*

"To those who desire to read for themselves an authentic account of the Abyssinian martyrdoms, we cordially recommend the perusal of a brilliant little brochure, entitled 'Abyssinia: its Past, Present, and Probable Future,' from the facile pen of the Rev. Dr. Margoliouth. It is a book that will repay an attentive consideration."—*Bell's Weekly Messenger.*

II.
THE HAIDAD; A HARVEST THANKSGIVING SERMON.
With Preface and Appendices intended for careful perusal. Price 1s.

"I beg to thank you for your learned sermon, entitled 'Haidad.' Your exposition of that word is a very interesting one, and it seems to have the marks of probability, and to open out a view of joyful religious associations, especially in connection with Harvest Thanksgiving."—*Extract from a Letter of the Venerable Archdeacon Wordsworth.*

"A learned Harvest Sermon."—*The Guardian.*

"In the discourse will be found much matter of interest to those who wish to gain an insight into that abstruse subject, the metrical, or poetical anatomy of the Psalms in the original Hebrew."—*The Musical Standard.*

III.
THE SPIRIT OF PROPHECY: being an Exposition,
in Four Sermons, on Revelation i. 7, xxii. 20. Preached on the Mornings of the Sundays in Advent, 1863, with Appendices. Price 2s. 6d.

"The author displays, with some power, the sublime incidents of the second coming of our Lord."—*Church Review.*

"We shall always be glad to receive from his pen Expositions of Holy Writ, at once so full of learning, and so free from extravagances as those contained in the work before us."—*Clerical Journal.*

WORKS BY THE SAME AUTHOR.

IV.

ENGLAND'S CROWN OF REJOICING: a Sermon preached on the Sunday before the Marriage of the Prince of Wales. With an Appendix: being a Translation of the Hebrew Poem presented to the late Prince Consort, at the Baptism of H.R.H. the Prince of Wales. Price 1s.

"This is a sermon extremely appropriate to the occasion on which it was preached, from a text of singular beauty and significance."—*Literary Churchman.*

V.

THE TRUE LIGHT: a Farewell Sermon preached on the evening of St. Bartholomew's Day, in the Parish Church of Wyton, Hunts, on retiring from the spiritual charge of the Parish. Price 6d.

"We do not know when we have heard any one speak out more plainly on the sin and danger of schism than does Dr. Margoliouth. * * * We thank him for giving the weight of his name to the present protest against schism on the part of the Clergy."—*The Clerical Journal.*

VI.

THE END OF THE LAW: Two Sermons preached at the Church of St. Edmund-the-King, Lombard Street. To which is added A LETTER, with numerous Notes, to the Rev. William J. C. Lindsay, B.A., Rector of Llanvaches, Monmouthshire; being a Preliminary Examination of the "Essays and Reviews." *Rivingtons.*

"A valuable work."—*Bishop of Rochester.*

"A learned and useful work—profitable to the Church at the present time."—*Rev. Dr. M'Caul.*

"A most well-timed and important work, calculated to do immediate good. Interesting and *zweckmässig.*"—*Rev. Dr. Jelf.*

"Your strictures on the 'Essays and Reviews' are appropriate and well-timed."—*Rev. Thomas Hartwell Horne.*

"No one can peruse a single page of this admirable work without being struck at once by its profundity as well as its clearness . . . . . The style is easy, lucid, and pleasant to read, even when expounding matters which are usually served up as *pièces de resistance* for the delectation of savans alone."—*Weekly Messenger.*

VII.

THE GOSPEL AND ITS MISSION. *Second Edition.*

"It is an admirable Sermon."—*Rev. Dr. Marsh.*

WORKS BY THE SAME AUTHOR.

VIII.
SACRED MINSTRELSY. A Lecture on Biblical and Post-Biblical Hebrew Music.

"A great deal of interesting matter is given in these pages. The Jewish airs will please the lovers of music."—*Clerical Journal.*

IX.
THE QUARREL OF GOD'S COVENANT. A Fast-Day Sermon. *Wertheim, Macintosh, and Hunt.*

X.
THE LORD'S ANOINTED. A Coronation Sermon,
preached in the British Chapel at Moscow, on the Sunday before the enthronement of Alexander II. *Booth.*

"May claim attention as a historical document, as well as a pulpit discourse."—*Literary Gazette.*

XI.
THE PENITENTIAL HYMN of JUDAH and ISRAEL
after the SPIRIT: an Exposition of Isaiah liii. *Second Edition. Longman and Co.*

Extract from a letter to the Author, by the late Bishop of Kildare:—
"My dear Margoliouth,—I return the two last of a series of Sermons which it would be unjust to withhold from the public at large," &c.

"Able, learned, and most profitable throughout; to the scholar it will be most interesting."—*Presbyterian Review.*

"The author's whole aim is to demonstrate its vital importance, for which purpose he takes it verse by verse, and comments upon each expression critically, historically, polemically, and practically . . . . . We feel that we are quite safe in commending these Lectures to the attentive perusal of all who are interested in this most wonderful prophecy."—*English Review.*

XII.
GENUINE REPENTANCE, and its EFFECTS. An
Exposition of the Fourteenth Chapter of Hosea. *Longman and Co.*

"You have selected a very interesting portion of Scripture, and one peculiarly suited to our moral and political state; and I cannot doubt of the effect that address will have upon your hearers."—*One of the Last Letters of the late Chancellor Raikes, of Chester, to the Author.*

"The discourses are earnest and practical."—*The Literary Gazette.*

WORKS BY THE SAME AUTHOR.

XIII.

THE APOSTOLIC TRIPLE BENEDICTION. A
Farewell Sermon, preached at St. Bartholomew's Church, Salford.

XIV.

HOLMFIRTH'S SOLEMN VOICE. A Sermon preached
in St. Bartholomew's Church, Salford, in behalf of the Sufferers from the calamitous visitation of Holmfirth. *Wertheim and Macintosh.*

XV.

THE HISTORY of the JEWS in GREAT BRITAIN.
In Three Vols. Post 8vo. *Richard Bentley.*

"The minute and patient research here bestowed on the History of the Jews in England has brought to light a mass of curious information, of which few have any idea. The work is one of real value, in more ways than one; especially as containing fragments of history almost inaccessible."
—*Presbyterian Review.*

"These volumes are invested with great historical value and importance."
—*Caledonian Mercury.*

"A very complete and interesting History of the Jews in England. The Author writes with candour and impartiality."—*Weekly Chronicle.*

XVI.

A PILGRIMAGE TO THE LAND OF MY FATHERS.
Two Vols. 8vo. With numerous Illustrations. *Richard Bentley.*

"The Letters which he (Mr. M. M.) addressed to me were replete with interesting information. The friends to whom I communicated them, read them with as much pleasure as I had done; and I believe him not only to be singularly qualified to draw out and discover what is curious in the countries that he visited, but likewise very happy in his manner of describing them."—*The Worshipful and Rev. Chancellor Raikes.*

"So ends our review of a work which has entertained us with a variety of topics, treated in an original way."—*Literary Gazette.*

"The work abounds with curious details concerning the condition and opinions of the Jewish populations of the various countries in Europe, Asia, and Africa, which the Author visited. Some of the disclosures, too, are as astounding and romantic as anything in Mr. Disraeli's fictions, and with the additional advantage of being not inventions but truths....... Of the more learned portions of the work, its critical and antiquarian discussions, we despair of giving an adequate account. They embrace a great variety of subjects, and are highly creditable to the Author's learning and ability."—*Daily News.*

"It is replete with information as varied as it is valuable, as curious as it is attractive."—*Britannia.*

"He appears to be thoroughly conversant with Hebrew literature, and his notices of Hebrew poetry, and occasional specimens of Hebrew music, are curious."—*Examiner.*

XVII.

THE FUNDAMENTAL PRINCIPLES OF MODERN JUDAISM INVESTIGATED. One Vol. 8vo. *Wertheim and Macintosh.*

"Your luminous book, which suggests a most valuable alteration in the course hitherto pursued by students of Theology, has not yet been a sufficient time before the public to excite attention. . . . . Your investigation of Modern Judaism I have read several times throughout with great attention. That work, with Mr. Chancellor Raikes' Preface, and your short Memoir, form a compendium of much value to Theological Students, because it brings together one whole subject of Talmudical learning, which they have had to collect from different authors."—*Extract from a Letter of the late Bishop of Kildare to the Author.*

XVIII.

ISRAEL'S ORDINANCES EXAMINED. 8vo. *Wertheim and Macintosh.*

"We do not know any one whose reply we should look for with more interest than Mr. Margoliouth's; and on the perusal of his little pamphlet, we found it just as happy in its spirit as it is conclusive in its arguments."—*Christian Examiner.*

&c., &c., &c., &c.

WORKS READY FOR PRESS THESE MANY YEARS, BY THE SAME AUTHOR.

The Hebrew Old Testament,

WITH

CRITICAL, PHILOLOGICAL, HISTORICAL, POLEMICAL, AND EXPOSITORY ENGLISH COMMENTS;

THE PRINCIPAL PORTIONS OF WHICH ARE ORIGINAL.

In Five Quarto Volumes.

The Author humbly trusts that, with the blessing of God, the work which he has been permitted to finish will not only prove useful to the advanced Theological Student, but *also prove an important auxiliary to the ordinary Bible reader, who may be altogether unacquainted with the Sacred tongue.*

The production of this work has been one of the principal objects of the Author's life; he has diligently studied the writings of Moses and the prophets in their original tongue, with a view to their elucidation. During his various travels in the East, the West, and the North, he has ever borne in mind his great enterprise, *viz.*, the illustration of the "Scriptures of Truth."

A great number of new references have been added in the margin of this work, and the inapplicable ones discarded. A considerable number of new readings have been discovered, which make many passages, hitherto obscure, clear and intelligible.

The Author has already spent upwards of Six Thousand Pounds sterling on the preparation of this work. The enterprise proved the cause of protracted illness, misfortunes, and disappointments to him, all of which conspired in putting the publication of it, for a time at least, in abeyance.

THE HISTORY OF THE JEWS FROM THE GREAT DISPERSION to A.D. 1860. Twelve Vols. 8vo.

THE WHOLE PLAN OF POST-BIBLICAL JUDAISM.

ESSAYS ON THE POETRY AND MUSIC OF THE HEBREWS, BIBLICAL AND POST-BIBLICAL. Two Vols.

MISCELLANEOUS LECTURES. Two Vols. 8vo.

&c., &c., &c.

39 Paternoster Row, E.C.
London: *April* 1869.

GENERAL LIST OF WORKS

PUBLISHED BY

Messrs. LONGMANS, GREEN, READER, and DYER.

Arts, Manufactures, &c. 12	Miscellaneous and Popular Metaphysical Works 6
Astronomy, Meteorology, Popular Geography, &c. 7	Natural History and Popular Science 8
Biography and Memoirs 3	
Chemistry, Medicine, Surgery, and the Allied Sciences 9	Poetry and The Drama 18
Commerce, Navigation, and Mercantile Affairs 19	Religious and Moral Works 13
	Rural Sports, &c. 19
Criticism, Philology, &c. 4	Travels, Voyages, &c. 16
Fine Arts and Illustrated Editions 11	Works of Fiction 17
Historical Works 1	Works of Utility and General Information 20
Index ....21—24	

Historical Works.

Lord Macaulay's Works. Complete and uniform Library Edition. Edited by his Sister, Lady Trevelyan. 8 vols. 8vo. with Portrait, price £5 5s. cloth, or £8 8s. bound in tree-calf by Rivière.

The History of England from the fall of Wolsey to the Death of Elizabeth. By James Anthony Froude, M.A. late Fellow of Exeter College, Oxford. Vols. I. to X. in 8vo. price £7 2s. cloth.

Vols. I. to IV. the Reign of Henry VIII. Fourth Edition, 54s.

Vols. V. and VI. the Reigns of Edward VI. and Mary. Third Edition, 28s.

Vols. VII. & VIII. the Reign of Elizabeth. Vols. I. & II. Fourth Edition, 28s.

Vols. IX. and X. the Reign of Elizabeth. Vols. III. and IV. 32s.

The History of England from the Accession of James II. By Lord Macaulay.

Library Edition, 5 vols. 8vo. £4.
Cabinet Edition, 8 vols. post 8vo. 48s.
People's Edition, 4 vols. crown 8vo. 16s.

An Essay on the History of the English Government and Constitution, from the Reign of Henry VII. to the Present Time. By John Earl Russell. Fourth Edition, revised. Crown 8vo. 6s.

On Parliamentary Government in England: its Origin, Development, and Practical Operation. By Alpheus Todd, Librarian of the Legislative Asembly of Canada. Vol. I. 8vo. 16s.

The History of England during the Reign of George the Third. By the Right Hon. W. N. Massey. Cabinet Edition. 4 vols. post 8vo. 24s.

The Constitutional History of England since the Accession of George III. 1760—1860. By Sir Thomas Erskine May, K.C.B. Second Edit. 2 vols. 8vo. 33s.

History of the Reform Bills of 1866 and 1867. By Homersham Cox, M.A. Barrister-at-Law. 8vo. 7s. 6d.

Ancient Parliamentary Elections: a History shewing how Parliaments were Constituted, and Representatives of the People Elected in Ancient Times. By the same Author. 8vo. 8s. 6d.

Whig and Tory Administrations during the Last Thirteen Years. By the same Author. 8vo. 5s.

Historical Studies. I. On Precursors of the French Revolution; II. Studies from the History of the Seventeenth Century; III. Leisure Hours of a Tourist. By Herman Merivale, M.A. 8vo. 12s. 6d.

A

Lectures on the History of England, from the Earliest Times to the Death of King Edward II. By WILLIAM LONGMAN. With Maps and Illustrations. 8vo. 15s.

The History of the Life and Times of Edward the Third. By WILLIAM LONGMAN. With 9 Maps, 8 Plates, and 16 Woodcuts. 2 vols. 8vo. 28s.

History of Civilization in England and France, Spain and Scotland. By HENRY THOMAS BUCKLE. Fifth Edition of the entire work, with a complete INDEX. 3 vols. crown 8vo. 24s.

Realities of Irish Life. By W. STEUART TRENCH, Land Agent in Ireland to the Marquess of Lansdowne, the Marquess of Bath, and Lord Digby. With Illustrations from Drawings by the Author's Son, J TOWNSEND TRENCH. Third Edition, with 30 Plates. 8vo. 21s.

Journals, Conversations, and Essays relating to Ireland. By NASSAU WILLIAM SENIOR. Second Edition. 2 vols. post 8vo. 21s.

Modern Ireland: its Vital Questions, Secret Societies, and Government. By an ULSTERMAN. Post 8vo. 6s.

Ireland in 1868 the Battle-Field for English Party Strife: its Grievances, Real and Factitious; Remedies, Abortive or Mischievous. By GERALD FITZGIBBON. Second Edition. 8vo. 8s. 6d.

An Illustrated History of Ireland, from the Earliest Period to the Year of Catholic Emancipation. By MARY F. CUSACK. Second Edition, revised and enlarged. 8vo. 18s. 6d.

The History of India, from the Earliest Period to the close of Lord Dalhousie's Administration. By JOHN CLARK MARSHMAN. 3 vols. crown 8vo. 22s. 6d.

Indian Polity: a View of the System of Administration in India. By Major GEORGE CHESNEY, Fellow of the University of Calcutta. 8vo. with Map, 21s.

History of the French in India, from the Founding of Pondichery in 1674 to its Capture in 1761. By Lieutenant-Colonel G. B. MALLESON, Bengal Staff Corps. 8vo. 16s.

Democracy in America. By ALEXIS DE TOCQUEVILLE. Translated by HENRY REEVE. 2 vols. 8vo. 21s.

History of Grant's Campaign for the Capture of Richmond, 1864-1865; with an Outline of the Previous Course of the American Civil War. By JOHN CANNON. Post 8vo. 12s. 6d.

Waterloo Lectures: a Study of the Campaign of 1815. By Colonel CHARLES C. CHESNEY, R.E. late Professor of Military Art and History in the Staff College. New Edition, nearly ready.

The Oxford Reformers of 1498; being a History of the Fellow-work of John Colet, Erasmus, and Thomas More. By FREDERIC SEEBOHM. 8vo. 12s.

History of the Reformation in Europe in the Time of Calvin. By J. H. MERLE D'AUBIGNÉ, D.D. VOLS. I. and II. 8vo. 28s. VOL. III. 12s. VOL. IV. price 16s. and VOL. V. price 16s.

The History of France, from Clovis and Charlemagne to the Accession of Napoleon III. By EYRE EVANS CROWE. 5 vols. 8vo. £4 13s.

The History of Greece. By C. THIRLWALL, D.D. Lord Bishop of St. David's. 8 vols. fcp. 28s.

The Tale of the Great Persian War, from the Histories of Herodotus. By GEORGE W. COX, M.A. late Scholar of Trin. Coll. Oxon. Fcp. 3s. 6d.

Greek History from Themistocles to Alexander, in a Series of Lives from Plutarch. Revised and arranged by A. H. CLOUGH. Fcp. with 44 Woodcuts, 6s.

Critical History of the Language and Literature of Ancient Greece. By WILLIAM MURE, of Caldwell. 5 vols. 8vo. £3 9s.

History of the Literature of Ancient Greece. By Professor K. L. MÜLLER. Translated by LEWIS and DONALDSON. 3 vols. 8vo. 21s.

History of the City of Rome from its Foundation to the Sixteenth Century of the Christian Era. By THOMAS H. DYER, LL.D. 8vo. with 2 Maps, 15s.

History of the Romans under the Empire. By C. MERIVALE, LL.D. Chaplain to the Speaker. 8 vols. post 8vo. price 48s.

The Fall of the Roman Republic: a Short History of the Last Century of the Commonwealth. By the same Author. 12mo. 7s. 6d.

The Conversion of the Roman Empire; the Boyle Lectures for the year 1864, delivered at the Chapel Royal, Whitehall. By the same Author. Second Edition. 8vo. 8s. 6d.

The Conversion of the Northern Nations; the Boyle Lectures for 1865. By the same Author. 8vo. 8s. 6d.

History of the Norman Kings of England, drawn from a New Collation of the Contemporary Chronicles by THOMAS COBBE, of the Inner Temple, Barrister-at-Law. 1 vol. 8vo. [*Nearly ready.*

History of European Morals from Augustus to Charlemagne. By W. E. H. LECKY, M.A. 2 vols. 8vo. price 28s.

History of the Rise and Influence of the Spirit of Rationalism in Europe. By the same Author. Third Edition. 2 vols. 8vo. price 25s.

God in History; or, the Progress of Man's Faith in the Moral Order of the World. By the late Baron BUNSEN. Translated from the German by SUSANNA WINKWORTH; with a Preface by the Dean of Westminster. VOLS. I. and II. 8vo. 30s.

Socrates and the Socratic Schools. Translated from the German of Dr. E. ZELLER, with the Author's approval, by the Rev. OSWALD J. REICHEL, B.C.L. and M.A. Crown 8vo. 8s. 6d.

The History of Philosophy, from Thales to Comte. By GEORGE HENRY LEWES. Third Edition, rewritten and enlarged. 2 vols. 8vo. 30s.

The English Reformation. By F. C. MASSINGBERD, M.A. Chancellor of Lincoln. 4th Edition, revised. Fcp. 7s. 6d.

Egypt's Place in Universal History; an Historical Investigation. By BARON BUNSEN, D.C.L. Translated by C. H. COTTRELL, M.A. with Additions by S. BIRCH, LL.D. 5 vols. 8vo. £8 14s. 6d.

Maunder's Historical Treasury; comprising a General Introductory Outline of Universal History, and a Series of Separate Histories. Fcp. 10s. 6d.

Historical and Chronological Encyclopædia, presenting in a brief and convenient form Chronological Notices of all the Great Events of Universal History. By B. B. WOODWARD, F.S.A. Librarian to the Queen. [*In the press.*

Critical and Historical Essays contributed to the *Edinburgh Review* by the Right Hon. Lord MACAULAY :—
LIBRARY EDITION, 3 vols. 8vo. 36s.
TRAVELLER'S EDITION, in 1 vol. 21s.
CABINET EDITION, 4 vols. 24s.
PEOPLE'S EDITION, 2 vols. crown 8vo. 8s

History of the Christian Church, from the Ascension of Christ to the Conversion of Constantine. By E. BURTON, D.D late Regius Prof. of Divinity in the University of Oxford. Fcp. 3s. 6d.

History of the Early Church, from the First Preaching of the Gospel to the Council of Nicæa, A.D. 325. By the Author of 'Amy Herbert.' Fcp. 4s. 6d.

Biography and *Memoirs.*

Dictionary of General Biography; containing Concise Memoirs and Notices of the most Eminent Persons of all Countries, from the Earliest Ages to the Present Time. Edited by WILLIAM L. R. CATES. 8vo. price 21s.

Memoirs of Baron Bunsen, drawn chiefly from Family Papers by his Widow, FRANCES Baroness BUNSEN. Second Edition, abridged; with 2 Portraits and 4 Woodcuts. 2 vols. post 8vo. 21s.

Life and Correspondence of Richard Whately, D.D. late Archbishop of Dublin. By E. JANE WHATELY. Popular Edition, with Portrait. Crown 8vo. 7s. 6d.

Life of the Duke of Wellington. By the Rev. G. R. GLEIG, M.A. Popular Edition, carefully revised; with copious Additions. Crown 8vo. with Portrait, 5s.

Father Mathew: a Biography. By JOHN FRANCIS MAGUIRE, M.P. Popular Edition, with Portrait. Crown 8vo. 3s. 6d.

History of my Religious Opinions. By J. H. NEWMAN, D.D. Being the Substance of Apologia pro Vitâ Suâ. Post 8vo. price 6s.

Letters and Life of Francis Bacon, including all his Occasional Works. Collected and edited, with a Commentary, by J. SPEDDING, Trin. Coll. Cantab. VOLS. I. & II. 8vo. 24s. VOLS. III. & IV. 24s.

Life of Pastor Fliedner, Founder of the Deaconesses' Institution at Kaiserswerth. Translated from the German by CATHERINE WINKWORTH. Fcp. 8vo. with Portrait, price 3s. 6d.

The Life of Franz Schubert, translated from the German of K. VON HELLBORN by A. D. COLERIDGE, M.A. late Fellow of King's College, Cambridge. With an Appendix by G. GROVE. 2 vols post 8vo. with Portrait, 21s.

Felix Mendelssohn's Letters from *Italy and Switzerland,* and *Letters* from 1833 to 1847, translated by Lady WALLACE. With Portrait. 2 vols. crown 8vo. 5s. each.

Reminiscences of Felix Mendelssohn-Bartholdy. By ELISE POLKO. Translated from the German by Lady WALLACE; with additional Letters addressed to English Correspondents. Post 8vo. with Portrait and View, 10s. 6d.

Captain Cook's Life, Voyages, and Discoveries. 18mo. Woodcuts. 2s. 6d.

Life of Sir John Richardson, C.B. sometime Inspector of Naval Hospitals and Fleets. By the Rev. JOHN MCILRAITH. Fcp. 8vo. with Portrait, 5s.

Memoirs of Sir Henry Havelock, K.C.B. By JOHN CLARK MARSHMAN. Cabinet Edition, with Portrait. Crown 8vo. price 5s.

Essays on Educational Reformers; the Jesuits, Locke, J. J. Rousseau, Pestalozzi, Jacotot, &c. By the Rev. R. H. QUICK, M.A. Trin. Coll. Cantab. Post 8vo. price 7s. 6d.

Essays, Biographical and Critical. By A. L. MEISSNER, Ph.D. Professor of Modern Languages in Queen's College, Belfast, and in the Queen's University in Ireland. [*Nearly ready.*

Faraday as a Discoverer. By JOHN TYNDALL, LL.D. F.R.S. Crown 8vo. with Two Portraits, 6s.

George Petrie, LL.D. M.R.I.A. &c. formerly President of the Royal Hibernian Academy; his Life and Labours in Art and Archæology. By WILLIAM STOKES, M.D. &c. Physician-in-Ordinary to the Queen in Ireland. 8vo. 12s. 6d.

Essays in Ecclesiastical Biography. By the Right Hon. Sir J. STEPHEN, LL.D. Cabinet Edition. Crown 8vo. 7s. 6d.

The Earls of Granard: a Memoir of the Noble Family of Forbes. Written by Admiral the Hon. JOHN FORBES, and Edited by GEORGE ARTHUR HASTINGS, present Earl of Granard, K.P. 8vo. 10s.

Vicissitudes of Families. By Sir J. BERNARD BURKE, C.B. Ulster King of Arms. New Edition, remodelled and enlarged. 2 vols. crown 8vo. 21s.

Lives of the Tudor Princesses, including Lady Jane Grey and her Sisters. By AGNES STRICKLAND, Author of 'Lives of the Queens of England.' Post 8vo. with Portrait, &c. 12s. 6d.

Maunder's Biographical Treasury. Thirteenth Edition, reconstructed and partly re-written, with above 1,000 additional Memoirs, by W. L. R. CATES. Fcp. 10s. 6d.

Criticism, Philosophy, Polity, &c.

On Representative Government. By JOHN STUART MILL. Third Edition. 8vo. 9s. crown 8vo. 2s.

On Liberty. By the same Author. Fourth Edition. Post 8vo. 7s. 6d. crown 8vo. 1s. 4d.

Principles of Political Economy. By the same. Sixth Edition. 2 vols. 8vo. 30s. or in 1 vol. crown 8vo. 5s.

Utilitarianism. By the same. 3d Edit. 8vo. 5s.

Dissertations and Discussions. By the same Author. 3 vols. 8vo. 36s.

Examination of Sir W. Hamilton's Philosophy, and of the principal Philosophical Questions discussed in his Writings. By the same. Third Edition. 8vo. 16s.

A System of Logic, Ratiocinative and Inductive. By the same. Seventh Edition. 2 vols. 8vo. 25s.

Inaugural Address delivered to the University of St. Andrews. By JOHN STUART MILL, 8vo. 5s.; crown 8vo. 1s.

Analysis of the Phenomena of the Human Mind. By JAMES MILL. A New Edition, with Notes, Illustrative and Critical, by ALEXANDER BAIN, ANDREW FINDLATER, and GEORGE GROTE. Edited, with additional Notes, by JOHN STUART MILL. 2 vols. 8vo. price 28s.

The Elements of Political Economy. By HENRY DUNNING MACLEOD, M.A. Barrister-at-Law. 8vo. 16s.

A Dictionary of Political Economy; Biographical, Bibliographical, Historical, and Practical. By the same Author. VOL. I. royal 8vo. 30s.

Lord Bacon's Works, collected and edited by R. L. ELLIS, M.A. J. SPEDDING, M.A. and D. D. HEATH. VOLS. I. to V. *Philosophical Works,* 5 vols. 8vo. £4 6s. VOLS. VI. and VII. *Literary and Professional Works,* 2 vols. £1 16s.

Analysis of Mr. Mill's System of Logic. By W. STEBBING, M.A. Second Edition. 12mo. 3s. 6d.

The Institutes of Justinian; with English Introduction, Translation, and Notes. By T. C. SANDARS, M.A. Barrister-at-Law. Fourth Edition. 8vo. 15s.

The Ethics of Aristotle; with Essays and Notes. By Sir A. GRANT, Bart. M.A. LL.D. Second Edition, revised and completed. 2 vols. 8vo. price 28s.

Bacon's Essays, with Annotations. By R. WHATELY, D.D. late Archbishop of Dublin. Sixth Edition. 8vo. 10s. 6d.

Elements of Logic. By R. WHATELY, D.D. late Archbishop of Dublin. Ninth Edition. 8vo. 10s. 6d. crown 8vo. 4s. 6d.

Elements of Rhetoric. By the same Author. Seventh Edition. 8vo. 10s. 6d. crown 8vo. 4s. 6d.

English Synonymes. By E. JANE WHATELY. Edited by Archbishop WHATELY. 5th Edition. Fcp. 3s.

An Outline of the Necessary Laws of Thought: a Treatise on Pure and Applied Logic. By the Most Rev. W. THOMSON, D.D. Archbishop of York. Ninth Thousand. Crown 8vo. 5s. 6d.

The Election of Representatives, Parliamentary and Municipal; a Treatise. By THOMAS HARE, Barrister-at-Law. Third Edition, with Additions. Crown 8vo. 6s.

Speeches of the Right Hon. Lord MACAULAY, corrected by Himself. Library Edition, 8vo. 12s. People's Edition, crown 8vo. 3s. 6d.

Lord Macaulay's Speeches on Parliamentary Reform in 1831 and 1832. 16mo. price ONE SHILLING.

Walker's Pronouncing Dictionary of the English Language. Thoroughly revised Editions, by B. H. SMART. 8vo. 12s. 16mo. 6s.

A Dictionary of the English Language. By R. G. LATHAM, M.A. M.D. F.R.S. Founded on the Dictionary of Dr. S. JOHNSON, as edited by the Rev. H. J. TODD, with numerous Emendations and Additions. Publishing in 36 Parts, price 3s. 6d. each, to form 2 vols. 4to. VOL. I. in Two Parts, price £3 10s. now ready.

Thesaurus of English Words and Phrases, classified and arranged so as to facilitate the expression of Ideas, and assist in Literary Composition. By P. M. ROGET, M.D. New Edition. Crown 8vo. 10s. 6d.

The Debater; a Series of Complete Debates, Outlines of Debates, and Questions for Discussion. By F. ROWTON. Fcp. 6s.

Lectures on the Science of Language, delivered at the Royal Institution. By MAX MÜLLER, M.A. Fellow of All Souls College, Oxford. 2 vols. 8vo. FIRST SERIES, Fifth Edition, 12s. SECOND SERIES, Second Edition, 18s.

Chapters on Language. By F. W FARRAR, M.A. F.R.S. late Fellow of Trin. Coll. Cambridge. Crown 8vo. 8s. 6d.

A Book about Words. By G. H. GRAHAM, Author of 'English, or the Art of Composition,' 'English Synonymes,' 'English Grammar Practice,' 'English Style,' &c. Fcp. 8vo. [*Nearly ready.*

Manual of English Literature, Historical and Critical: with a Chapter on English Metres. By THOMAS ARNOLD, M.A. Second Edition. Crown 8vo. 7s. 6d.

Southey's Doctor, complete in One Volume, edited by the Rev. J. W. WARTER, B.D. Square crown 8vo. 12s. 6d.

Historical and Critical Commentary on the Old Testament; with a New Translation. By M. M. KALISCH, Ph.D. Vol. I. *Genesis*, 8vo. 18s. or adapted for the General Reader, 12s. Vol. II. *Exodus*, 15s. or adapted for the General Reader, 12s. Vol III. *Leviticus*, Part I. 15s. or adapted for the General Reader, 8s.

A Hebrew Grammar, with Exercises. By the same. Part I. *Outlines with Exercises*, 8vo. 12s. 6d. KEY, 5s. Part II. *Exceptional Forms and Constructions*, 12s. 6d.

A Latin-English Dictionary. By J. T. WHITE, D.D. of Corpus Christi College, and J. E. RIDDLE, M.A. of St. Edmund Hall, Oxford. 2 vols. 4to. pp. 2,128, price 42s.

White's College Latin-English Dictionary (Intermediate Size), abridged for the use of University Students from the Parent Work (as above). Medium 8vo. pp. 1,048, price 18s.

White's Junior Student's Complete Latin-English and English-Latin Dictionary Square 12mo. pp. 1,058, price 12s.

Separately { ENGLISH-LATIN, 5s. 6d.
{ LATIN-ENGLISH, 7s. 6d.

An English-Greek Lexicon, containing all the Greek Words used by Writers of good authority. By C. D. YONGE, B.A. New Edition. 4to. 21s.

Mr. Yonge's New Lexicon, English and Greek, abridged from his larger work (as above). Square 12mo. 8s. 6d.

A Greek-English Lexicon. Compiled by H. G. LIDDELL, D.D. Dean of Christ Church, and R. SCOTT, D.D. Master of Balliol. Fifth Edition. Crown 4to. 31s. 6d.

A Lexicon, Greek and English, abridged for Schools from LIDDELL and SCOTT's *Greek-English Lexicon.* Twelfth Edition. Square 12mo. 7s. 6d.

A Practical Dictionary of the French and English Languages. By Professor LÉON CONTANSEAU, many years French Examiner for Military and Civil Appointments, &c. New Edition, carefully revised. Post 8vo. 10s. 6d.

Contanseau's Pocket Dictionary, French and English, abridged from the above by the Author. New Edition. 18mo. price 3s. 6d.

A Sanskrit-English Dictionary, The Sanskrit words printed both in the original Devanagari and in Roman letters; with References to the Best Editions of Sanskrit Authors, and with Etymologies and comparisons of Cognate Words chiefly in Greek, Latin, Gothic, and Anglo-Saxon. Compiled by T. BENFEY. 8vo. 52s. 6d.

New Practical Dictionary of the German Language; German-English, and English-German. By the Rev. W. L. BLACKLEY, M.A. and Dr. CARL MARTIN FRIEDLÄNDER. Post 8vo. 7s. 6d.

Miscellaneous Works and *Popular Metaphysics.*

The Essays and Contributions of A. K. H. B. Author of 'The Recreations of a Country Parson.' Uniform Editions:—

Recreations of a Country Parson. FIRST and SECOND SERIES, 3s. 6d. each.

The Commonplace Philosopher in Town and Country. Crown 8vo. 3s. 6d.

Leisure Hours in Town; Essays Consolatory, Æsthetical, Moral, Social, and Domestic. Crown 8vo. 3s. 6d.

The Autumn Holidays of a Country Parson. Crown 8vo. 3s. 6d.

The Graver Thoughts of a Country Parson. FIRST and SECOND SERIES, crown 8vo. 3s. 6d. each.

Critical Essays of a Country Parson, selected from Essays contributed to *Fraser's Magazine.* Crown 8vo. 3s. 6d.

Sunday Afternoons at the Parish Church of a Scottish University City. Crown 8vo. 3s. 6d.

Lessons of Middle Age, with some Account of various Cities and Men. Crown 8vo. 3s. 6d.

Counsel and Comfort Spoken from a City Pulpit. Crown 8vo. 3s. 6d.

Changed Aspects of Unchanged Truths; Memorials of St. Andrews Sundays. Crown 8vo. 3s. 6d.

Short Studies on Great Subjects. By JAMES ANTHONY FROUDE, M.A. late Fellow of Exeter College, Oxford. Third Edition. 8vo. 12s.

Lord Macaulay's Miscellaneous Writings:—
LIBRARY EDITION, 2 vols. 8vo. Portrait, 21s.
PEOPLE'S EDITION, 1 vol. crown 8vo. 4s. 6d.

The Rev. Sydney Smith's Miscellaneous Works; including his Contributions to the *Edinburgh Review.* People's Edition, 2 vols. crown 8vo. 8s.

The Wit and Wisdom of the Rev. SYDNEY SMITH: a Selection of the most memorable Passages in his Writings and Conversation. 16mo. 5s.

Epigrams, Ancient and Modern: Humorous, Witty, Satirical, Moral and Panegyrical. Edited by Rev. JOHN BOOTH, B.A. Cambridge. Second Edition, revised and enlarged. Fcp. 7s. 6d.

The Folk-Lore of the Northern Counties of England and the Borders. By WILLIAM HENDERSON. With an Appendix on Household Stories by the Rev. S. BARING-GOULD. Crown 8vo. 9s. 6d.

The Silver Store. Collected from Mediæval Christian and Jewish Mines. By the Rev. S. BARING-GOULD, M.A. Crown 8vo. 6s.

The Pedigree of the English People; an Argument, Historical and Scientific, on the *Ethnology* of the English. By THOMAS NICHOLAS, M.A. Ph.D. 8vo. 16s.

The English and their Origin: a Prologue to authentic English History. By LUKE OWEN PIKE, M.A. Barrister-at-Law. 8vo. 9s.

Essays selected from Contributions to the *Edinburgh Review.* By HENRY ROGERS. Second Edition. 3 vols. fcp. 21s.

Reason and Faith, their Claims and Conflicts. By the same Author. New Edition, revised and extended. Crown 8vo. price 6s. 6d.

The Eclipse of Faith; or, a Visit to a Religious Sceptic. By HENRY ROGERS. Eleventh Edition. Fcp. 5s.

Defence of the Eclipse of Faith, by its Author. Third Edition. Fcp. 3s. 6d.

Selections from the Correspondence of R. E. H. Greyson. By the same Author. Third Edition. Crown 8vo. 7s. 6d.

Chips from a German Workshop; being Essays on the Science of Religion, and on Mythology, Traditions, and Customs. By MAX MÜLLER, M.A. Fellow of All Souls College, Oxford. Second Edition, revised, with an INDEX. 2 vols. 8vo. 21s.

Word Gossip; a Series of Familiar Essays on Words and their Peculiarities. By the Rev. W. L. BLACKLEY, M.A. Fcp. 8vo. 5s.

An Introduction to Mental Philosophy, on the Inductive Method. By J. D. MORELL, M.A. LL.D. 8vo. 12s.

Elements of Psychology, containing the Analysis of the Intellectual Powers. By the same Author. Post 8vo. 7s. 6d.

The Secret of Hegel: being the Hegelian System in Origin, Principle, Form, and Matter. By JAMES HUTCHISON STIRLING. 2 vols. 8vo. 28s.

The Senses and the Intellect. By ALEXANDER BAIN, M.A. Prof. of Logic in the Univ. of Aberdeen. Third Edition. 8vo. 15s.

The Emotions and the Will, by the same Author. Second Edition. 8vo. 15s.

On the Study of Character, including an Estimate of Phrenology. By the same Author. 8vo. 9s.

Mental and Moral Science: a Compendium of Psychology and Ethics. By the same Author. Second Edition. Crown 8vo. 10s. 6d.

The Philosophy of Necessity; or, Natural Law as applicable to Mental, Moral, and Social Science. By CHARLES BRAY. Second Edition. 8vo. 9s.

The Education of the Feelings and Affections. By the same Author. Third Edition. 8vo. 3s. 6d.

On Force, its Mental and Moral Correlates. By the same Author. 8vo. 5s.

Astronomy, Meteorology, Popular Geography, &c.

Outlines of Astronomy. By Sir J. F. W. HERSCHEL, Bart. M.A. Ninth Edition, revised; with Plates and Woodcuts. 8vo. 18s.

Saturn and its System. By RICHARD A. PROCTOR, B.A. late Scholar of St. John's Coll. Camb. and King's Coll. London. 8vo. with 14 Plates, 14s.

The Handbook of the Stars. By the same Author. Square fcp. 8vo. with 3 Maps, price 5s.

Celestial Objects for Common Telescopes. By T. W. WEBB, M.A. F.R.A.S. Second Edition, revised and enlarged, with Map of the Moon and Woodcuts. 16mo. price 7s. 6d.

Navigation and Nautical Astronomy (Practical, Theoretical, Scientific) for the use of Students and Practical Men. By J. MERRIFIELD, F.R.A.S. and H. EVERS. 8vo. 14s.

A General Dictionary of Geography, Descriptive, Physical, Statistical, and Historical; forming a complete Gazetteer of the World. By A. KEITH JOHNSTON, F.R.S.E. New Edition. 8vo. price 31s. 6d.

M'Culloch's Dictionary, Geographical, Statistical, and Historical, of the various Countries, Places, and principal Natural Objects in the World. Revised Edition, with the Statistical Information throughout brought up to the latest returns. By FREDERICK MARTIN. 4 vols. 8vo. with coloured Maps, £4 4s.

A Manual of Geography, Physical, Industrial, and Political. By W. HUGHES, F.R.G.S. Prof. of Geog. in King's Coll. and in Queen's Coll. Lond. With 6 Maps. Fcp. 7s. 6d.

The States of the River Plate: their Industries and Commerce, Sheep Farming, Sheep Breeding, Cattle Feeding, and Meat Preserving; the Employment of Capital, Land and Stock and their Values Labour and its Remuneration. By WILFRID LATHAM, Buenos Ayres. Second Edition. 8vo. 12s.

Maunder's Treasury of Geography, Physical, Historical, Descriptive, and Political. Edited by W. HUGHES, F.R.G.S. With 7 Maps and 16 Plates. Fcp. 10s. 6d

Physical Geography for Schools and General Readers. By M. F. MAURY LL.D. Fcp. with 2 Charts, 2s. 6d.

Natural History and Popular Science.

Elementary Treatise on Physics, Experimental and Applied, for the use of Colleges and Schools. Translated and Edited from GANOT's 'Éléments de Physique' (with the Author's sanction) by E. ATKINSON, Ph.D. F.C.S. New Edition, revised and enlarged; with a Coloured Plate and 620 Woodcuts. Post 8vo. 15s.

The Elements of Physics or Natural Philosophy. By NEIL ARNOTT, M.D. F.R.S. Physician-Extraordinary to the Queen. Sixth Edition, re-written and completed. 2 Parts, 8vo. 21s.

Dove's Law of Storms, considered in connexion with the ordinary Movements of the Atmosphere. Translated by R. H. SCOTT, M.A. T.C.D. 8vo. 10s. 6d.

Sound: a Course of Eight Lectures delivered at the Royal Institution of Great Britain. By Professor JOHN TYNDALL, LL.D. F.R.S. Crown 8vo. with Portrait and Woodcuts, 9s.

Heat Considered as a Mode of Motion. By Professor JOHN TYNDALL, LL.D. F.R.S. Third Edition. Crown 8vo. with Woodcuts, 10s. 6d.

Light; its Influence on Life and Health. By FORBES WINSLOW, M.D. D.C.L. Oxon. (Hon.) Fcp. 8vo. 6s.

An Essay on Dew, and several Appearances connected with it. By W. C. WELLS. Edited, with Annotations, by L. P. CASELLA, F.R.A.S. and an Appendix by R. STRACHAN, F.M.S. 8vo. 5s.

A Treatise on the Action of Vis Inertiæ in the Ocean; with Remarks on the Abstract Nature of the Forces of Vis Inertiæ and Gravitation, and a New Theory of the Tides. By W. L. JORDAN, F.R.G.S. with Charts and Diagrams. 8vo. 14s.

A Treatise on Electricity, in Theory and Practice. By A. DE LA RIVE, Prof. in the Academy of Geneva. Translated by C. V. WALKER, F.R.S. 3 vols. 8vo. with Woodcuts, £3 13s.

A Preliminary Discourse on the Study of Natural Philosophy. By Sir JOHN F. W. HERSCHEL, Bart. Revised Edition, with Vignette Title. Fcp. 3s. 6d.

The Correlation of Physical Forces. By W. R. GROVE, Q.C. V.P.R.S. Fifth Edition, revised, and Augmented by a Discourse on Continuity. 8vo. 10s. 6d. The *Discourse on Continuity,* separately, price 2s. 6d.

Manual of Geology. By S. HAUGHTON, M.D. F.R.S. Fellow of Trin. Coll. and Prof. of Geol. in the Univ. of Dublin. Second Edition, with 66 Woodcuts. Fcp. 7s. 6d.

A Guide to Geology. By J. PHILLIPS, M.A. Prof. of Geol. in the Univ. of Oxford. Fifth Edition. Fcp. 4s.

The Student's Manual of Zoology and Comparative Physiology. By J. BURNEY YEO, M.B. Resident Medical Tutor and Lecturer on Animal Physiology in King's College, London. [*Nearly ready.*

Van Der Hoeven's Handbook of Zoology. Translated from the Second Dutch Edition by the Rev. W. CLARK, M.D. F.R.S. 2 vols. 8vo. with 24 Plates of Figures, 60s.

Professor Owen's Lectures on the Comparative Anatomy and Physiology of the Invertebrate Animals. Second Edition, with 235 Woodcuts. 8vo. 21s.

The Comparative Anatomy and Physiology of the Vertebrate Animals. By RICHARD OWEN, F.R.S. D.C.L. With 1,472 Woodcuts. 3 vols. 8vo. £3 13s. 6d.

The First Man and his Place in Creation, considered on the Principles of Common Sense from a Christian Point of View; with an Appendix on the Negro. By GEORGE MOORE, M.D. M.R.C.P.L. &c. Post 8vo. 8s. 6d.

The Primitive Inhabitants of Scandinavia. Containing a Description of the Implements, Dwellings, Tombs, and Mode of Living of the Savages in the North of Europe during the Stone Age. By SVEN NILSSON. Translated from the Third Edition; and edited, with an Introduction, by Sir JOHN LUBBOCK. With 16 Plates of Figures and 3 Woodcuts. 8vo. 18s.

Homes without Hands: a Description of the Habitations of Animals, classed according to their Principle of Construction. By Rev. J. G. WOOD, M.A. F.L.S. With about 140 Vignettes on Wood (20 full size of page). New Edition. 8vo. 21s.

Bible Animals; being an Account of the various Birds, Beasts, Fishes, and other Animals mentioned in the Holy Scriptures. By the Rev. J. G. WOOD, M.A. F.L.S. Copiously Illustrated with Original Designs, made under the Author's superintendence and engraved on Wood. In course of publication monthly, to be completed in Twenty Parts, price ONE SHILLING each.

The Harmonies of Nature and Unity of Creation. By Dr. G. HARTWIG. 8vo. with numerous Illustrations, 18s.

The Sea and its Living Wonders. By the same Author. Third Edition, enlarged. 8vo. with many Illustrations, 21s.

The Tropical World. By the same Author. With 8 Chromoxylographs and 172 Woodcuts. 8vo. 21s.

The Polar World: a Popular Description of Man and Nature in the Arctic and Antarctic Regions of the Globe. By the same Author. With 8 Chromoxylographs, 3 Maps, and 85 Woodcuts. 8vo. 21s.

Ceylon. By Sir J. EMERSON TENNENT, K.C.S. LL.D. 5th Edition; with Maps, &c. and 90 Wood Engravings. 2 vols. 8vo. £2 10s.

Manual of Corals and Sea Jellies. By J. R. GREENE, B.A. Edited by J. A. GALBRAITH, M.A. and S. HAUGHTON, M.D. Fcp. with 39 Woodcuts, 5s.

Manual of Sponges and Animalculæ; with a General Introduction on the Principles of Zoology. By the same Author and Editors. Fcp. with 16 Woodcuts, 2s.

Manual of the Metalloids. By J. APJOHN, M.D. F.R.S. and the same Editors. 2nd Edition. Fcp. with 38 Woodcuts, 7s. 6d.

A Familiar History of Birds. By E. STANLEY, D.D. late Lord Bishop of Norwich. Fcp. with Woodcuts, 3s. 6d.

Kirby and Spence's Introduction to Entomology, or Elements of the Natural History of Insects. Crown 8vo. 5s.

Maunder's Treasury of Natural History, or Popular Dictionary of Zoology. Revised and corrected by T. S. CONBOLD, M.D. Fcp. with 900 Woodcuts, 10s. 6d.

The Elements of Botany for Families and Schools. Tenth Edition, revised by THOMAS MOORE, F.L.S. Fcp. with 154 Woodcuts, 2s. 6d.

The Treasury of Botany, or Popular Dictionary of the Vegetable Kingdom; with which is incorporated a Glossary of Botanical Terms. Edited by J. LINDLEY, F.R.S. and T. MOORE, F.L.S. assisted by eminent Contributors. Pp. 1,274, with 274 Woodcuts and 20 Steel Plates. TWO PARTS, fcp. 8vo. 20s.

The British Flora; comprising the Phænogamous or Flowering Plants and the Ferns. By Sir W. J. HOOKER, K.H. and G. A. WALKER-ARNOTT, LL.D. 12mo. with 12 Plates, 14s. or coloured, 21s.

The Rose Amateur's Guide. By THOMAS RIVERS. New Edition. Fcp. 4s.

Loudon's Encyclopædia of Plants; comprising the Specific Character, Description, Culture, History, &c. of all the Plants found in Great Britain. With upwards of 12,000 Woodcuts. 8vo. 42s.

Maunder's Scientific and Literary Treasury; a Popular Encyclopædia of Science, Literature, and Art. New Edition, thoroughly revised and in great part re-written, with above 1,000 new articles, by J. Y. JOHNSON, Corr. M.Z.S. Fcp. 10s. 6d.

A Dictionary of Science, Literature, and Art. Fourth Edition, re-edited by the late W. T. BRANDE (the Author) and GEORGE W. COX, M.A. 3 vols. medium 8vo. price 63s. cloth.

The Quarterly Journal of Science. Edited by JAMES SAMUELSON and WILLIAM CROOKES, F.R.S. Published quarterly in January, April, July, and October. 8vo. with Illustrations, price 5s. each Number.

Chemistry, Medicine, Surgery, and *the Allied Sciences.*

A Dictionary of Chemistry and the Allied Branches of other Sciences. By HENRY WATTS, F.C.S. assisted by eminent Scientific and Practical Chemists. 5 vols. medium 8vo. price £7 3s.

Handbook of Chemical Analysis, adapted to the *Unitary System* of Notation. By F. T. CONINGTON, M.A. F.C.S. Post 8vo. 7s. 6d.

Conington's Tables of Qualitative Analysis, to accompany the above, 2s. 6d.

Elements of Chemistry, Theoretical and Practical. By WILLIAM A. MILLER, M.D. LL.D. Professor of Chemistry, King's College, London. Revised Edition. 3 vols. 8vo. £3.
PART I. CHEMICAL PHYSICS, 15s.
PART II. INORGANIC CHEMISTRY, 21s.
PART III. ORGANIC CHEMISTRY, 24s.

A Manual of Chemistry, Descriptive and Theoretical. By WILLIAM ODLING, M.B. F.R.S. PART I. 8vo. 9s. PART II. nearly ready.

A Course of Practical Chemistry, for the use of Medical Students. By W. ODLING, M.B. F.R.S. New Edition, with 70 new Woodcuts. Crown 8vo. 7s. 6d.

Lectures on Animal Chemistry Delivered at the Royal College of Physicians in 1865. By the same Author. Crown 8vo. 4s. 6d.

Chemical Notes for the Lecture Room. By THOMAS WOOD, F.C.S. 2 vols. crown 8vo. I. on Heat, &c. price 3s. 6d. II. on the Metals, price 5s.

The Diagnosis, Pathology, and Treatment of Diseases of Women; including the Diagnosis of Pregnancy. By GRAILY HEWITT, M.D. &c. President of the Obstetrical Society of London. Second Edition, enlarged; with 116 Woodcut Illustrations. 8vo. 24s.

Lectures on the Diseases of Infancy and Childhood. By CHARLES WEST, M.D. &c. 5th Edition, revised and enlarged. 8vo. 16s.

On the Surgical Treatment of Children's Diseases. By T. HOLMES, M.A. &c. late Surgeon to the Hospital for Sick Children. Second Edition, with 9 Plates and 112 Woodcuts. 8vo. 21s.

A System of Surgery, Theoretical and Practical, in Treatises by Various Authors. Edited by T. HOLMES, M.A. &c. Surgeon and Lecturer on Surgery at St. George's Hospital, and Surgeon-in-Chief to the Metropolitan Police. 4 vols. 8vo. £4 13s.

Lectures on the Principles and Practice of Physic. By Sir THOMAS WATSON, Bart. M.D. Physician-Extraordinary to the Queen. New Edition in preparation.

Lectures on Surgical Pathology. By J. PAGET, F.R.S. Surgeon-Extraordinary to the Queen. Edited by W. TURNER, M.B. New Edition in preparation.

On Chronic Bronchitis, especially as connected with Gout, Emphysema, and Diseases of the Heart. By E. HEADLAM GREENHOW, M.D. F.R.C.P. &c. 8vo. 7s. 6d.

A Treatise on the Continued Fevers of Great Britain. By C. MURCHISON. M.D. Physician and Lecturer on the Practice of Medicine, Middlesex Hospital. New Edition in preparation.

Clinical Lectures on Diseases of the Liver, Jaundice, and Abdominal Dropsy. By the same Author. Post 8vo. with 25 Woodcuts, 10s. 6d.

Anatomy, Descriptive and Surgical. By HENRY GRAY, F.R.S. With 410 Wood Engravings from Dissections. New Edition, by T. HOLMES, M.A. Cantab. Royal 8vo. 28s.

The House I Live in; or Popular Illustrations of the Structure and Functions of the Human Body. Edited by T. G. GIRTIN. New Edition, with 25 Woodcuts. 16mo. price 2s. 6d.

Outlines of Physiology, Human and Comparative. By JOHN MARSHALL, F.R.C.S. Professor of Surgery in University College, London, and Surgeon to the University College Hospital. 2 vols. crown 8vo. with 122 Woodcuts, 32s.

Physiological Anatomy and Physiology of Man. By the late R. B. TODD, M.D. F.R.S. and W. BOWMAN, F.R.S. of King's College. With numerous Illustrations. VOL. II. 8vo. 25s.

VOL. I. New Edition by Dr. LIONEL S. BEALE, F.R.S. in course of publication; PART I. with 8 Plates, 7s. 6d.

A Dictionary of Practical Medicine. By J. COPLAND, M.D. F.R.S. Abridged from the larger work by the Author, assisted by J. C. COPLAND, M.R.C.S. Pp. 1,560, in 8vo. price 36s.

The Works of Sir B. C. Brodie, Bart. collected and arranged by CHARLES HAWKINS, F.R.C.S.E. 3 vols. 8vo. with Medallion and Facsimile, 48s.

The Theory of Ocular Defects and of Spectacles. Translated from the German of Dr. H. SCHEFFLER by R. B. CARTER, F.R.C.S. With Prefatory Notes and a Chapter of Practical Instructions. Post 8vo. 7s. 6d.

A Manual of Materia Medica and Therapeutics, abridged from Dr. PEREIRA's *Elements* by F. J. FARRE, M.D. assisted by R. BENTLEY, M.R.C.S. and by R. WARINGTON, F.R.S. 1 vol. 8vo. with 90 Woodcuts, 21s.

Thomson's Conspectus of the British Pharmacopœia. Twenty-fifth Edition, corrected by E. LLOYD BIRKETT, M.D. 18mo. 6s.

Manual of the Domestic Practice of Medicine. By W. B. KESTEVEN, F.R.C.S.E. Third Edition, thoroughly revised, with Additions. Fcp. 5s.

Essays on Physiological Subjects. By GILBERT W. CHILD, M.D. F.L.S. F.C.S of Exeter College, Oxford. 8vo. 5s.

Gymnasts and Gymnastics. By JOHN H. HOWARD, late Professor of Gymnastics, Comm. Coll. Ripponden. Second Edition, revised and enlarged, with 135 Woodcuts of Apparatus, &c. Cr. 8vo. 10s. 6d.

The Fine Arts, and Illustrated Editions.

Materials for a History of Oil Painting. By Sir CHARLES LOCKE EASTLAKE, sometime President of the Royal Academy. VOL. II. 8vo. 14s.

Half-Hour Lectures on the History and Practice of the Fine and Ornamental Arts. By. W. B. SCOTT. Second Edition. Crown 8vo. with 50 Woodcut Illustrations, 8s. 6d.

Lectures on the History of Modern Music, delivered at the Royal Institution. By JOHN HULLAH. FIRST COURSE, with Chronological Tables, post 8vo. 6s. 6d. SECOND COURSE, the Transition Period, with 26 Specimens, 8vo. 16s.

The Chorale Book for England; a complete Hymn-Book in accordance with the Services and Festivals of the Church of England: the Hymns Translated by Miss C. WINKWORTH; the Tunes arranged by Prof. W. S. BENNETT and OTTO GOLDSCHMIDT. Fcp. 4to. 12s. 6d.

Congregational Edition. Fcp. 2s.

Six Lectures on Harmony. Delivered at the Royal Institution of Great Britain before Easter 1867. By G. A. MACFARREN. 8vo. 10s. 6d.

Sacred Music for Family Use; a selection of Pieces for One, Two, or more Voices, from the best Composers, Foreign and English. Edited by JOHN HULLAH. 1 vol. music folio, 21s.

Hullah's Part Music, New Edition, with Pianoforte Accompaniments. Just completed, an entirely New Edition of HULLAH's Two Collections of Part Music, Sacred Series and Secular Series, for Soprano, Alto, Tenor, and Bass, with Pianoforte Accompaniments, now first supplied. Each SERIES, Sacred and Secular, may now be had in TWO VOLUMES imperial 8vo. price 14s. cloth. The Score and the Voice Parts of each of the 133 pieces of which the Two Collections consist may also be had separately.

Lyra Germanica, the Christian Year. Translated by CATHERINE WINKWORTH; with 125 Illustrations on Wood drawn by J. LEIGHTON, F.S.A. Quarto, 21s.

Lyra Germanica. the Christian Life. Translated by CATHERINE WINKWORTH; with about 200 Woodcut Illustrations by J. LEIGHTON, F.S.A. and other Artists. Quarto, 21s.

The New Testament, illustrated with Wood Engravings after the Early Masters, chiefly of the Italian School. Crown 4to. 63s. cloth, gilt top; or £5 5s. morocco.

The Life of Man Symbolised by the Months of the Year in their Seasons and Phases. Text selected by RICHARD PIGOT. 25 Illustrations on Wood from Original Designs by JOHN LEIGHTON, F.S.A. Quarto, 42s.

Cats' and Farlie's Moral Emblems; with Aphorisms, Adages, and Proverbs of all Nations: comprising 121 Illustrations on Wood by J. LEIGHTON, F.S.A. with an appropriate Text by R. PIGOT. Imperial 8vo. 31s. 6d.

Shakspeare's Midsummer Night's Dream, illustrated with 24 Silhouettes or Shadow Pictures by P. KONEWKA, engraved on Wood by A. VOGEL. Folio, 31s. 6d

Shakspeare's Sentiments and Similes Printed in Black and Gold, and illuminated in the Missal style by HENRY NOEL HUMPHREYS. In massive covers, containing the Medallion and Cypher of Shakspeare. Square post 8vo. 21s.

Sacred and Legendary Art. By Mrs. JAMESON. With numerous Etchings and Woodcut Illustrations. 6 vols. square crown 8vo. price £5 15s. 6d. cloth, or £12 12s. bound in morocco by Rivière. To be had also in cloth only, in FOUR SERIES, as follows:—

Legends of the Saints and Martyrs. Fifth Edition, with 19 Etchings and 187 Woodcuts. 2 vols. square crown 8vo. 31s. 6d.

Legends of the Monastic Orders. Third Edition, with 11 Etchings and 88 Woodcuts. 1 vol. square crown 8vo. 21s.

Legends of the Madonna. Third Edition, with 27 Etchings and 165 Woodcuts. 1 vol. square crown 8vo. 21s.

The History of Our Lord, as exemplified in Works of Art. Completed by Lady EASTLAKE. Revised Edition, with 13 Etchings and 281 Woodcuts. 2 vols. square crown 8vo. 42s.

Arts, Manufactures, &c.

Drawing from Nature; a Series of Progressive Instructions in Sketching, from Elementary Studies to Finished Views, with Examples from Switzerland and the Pyrenees. By GEORGE BARNARD, Professor of Drawing at Rugby School. With 18 Lithographic Plates and 108 Wood Engravings. Imp. 8vo. 25s. or in Three Parts, royal 8vo. 7s. 6d. each.

Gwilt's Encyclopædia of Architecture. Fifth Edition, with Alterations and considerable Additions, by WYATT PAPWORTH. Additionally illustrated with nearly 400 Wood Engravings by O. JEWITT, and upwards of 100 other new Woodcuts. 8vo. 52s. 6d.

Italian Sculptors: being a History of Sculpture in Northern, Southern, and Eastern Italy. By C. C. PERKINS. With 30 Etchings and 13 Wood Engravings. Imperial 8vo. 42s.

Tuscan Sculptors, their Lives, Works, and Times. By the same Author. With 45 Etchings and 28 Woodcuts from Original Drawings and Photographs. 2 vols. imperial 8vo. 63s.

Original Designs for Wood-Carving, with Practical Instructions in the Art. By A. F. B. With 20 Plates of Illustrations engraved on Wood. Quarto, 18s.

Hints on Household Taste in Furniture, Upholstery, and other Details. By CHARLES L. EASTLAKE, Architect. With about 90 Illustrations. Square crown 8vo. 18s.

The Engineer's Handbook; explaining the principles which should guide the young Engineer in the Construction of Machinery. By C. S. LOWNDES. Post 8vo. 5s.

Lathes and Turning, Simple, Mechanical, and Ornamental. By W. HENRY NORTHCOTT. With about 240 Illustrations on Steel and Wood. 8vo. 18s.

The Elements of Mechanism. By T. M. GOODEVE, M.A. Prof. of Mechanics at the R. M. Acad. Woolwich. Second Edition, with 217 Woodcuts. Post 8vo. 6s. 6d.

Handbook of Practical Telegraphy, published with the sanction of the Chairman and Directors of the Electric and International Telegraph Company, and adopted by the Department of Telegraphs for India. By R. S. CULLEY. Third Edition. 8vo. 12s. 6d.

Ure's Dictionary of Arts, Manufactures, and Mines. Sixth Edition, chiefly re-written and greatly enlarged by ROBERT HUNT, F.R.S. assisted by numerous Contributors eminent in Science and the Arts, and familiar with Manufactures. With 2,000 Woodcuts. 3 vols. medium 8vo. £4 14s. 6d.

Treatise on Mills and Millwork. By W. FAIRBAIRN, C.E. F.R.S. With 18 Plates and 322 Woodcuts. 2 vols. 8vo. 32s.

Useful Information for Engineers. By the same Author. FIRST, SECOND, and THIRD SERIES, with many Plates and Woodcuts. 3 vols. crown 8vo. 10s. 6d. each.

The Application of Cast and Wrought Iron to Building Purposes. By the same Author. Third Edition, with 6 Plates and 118 Woodcuts. 8vo. 16s.

Iron Ship Building, its History and Progress, as comprised in a Series of Experimental Researches on the Laws of Strain; the Strengths, Forms, and other conditions of the Material; and an Inquiry into the Present and Prospective State of the Navy, including the Experimental Results on the Resisting Powers of Armour Plates and Shot at High Velocities. By W. FAIRBAIRN, C.E. F.R.S. With 4 Plates and 130 Woodcuts, 8vo. 18s.

Encyclopædia of Civil Engineering, Historical, Theoretical, and Practical. By E. CRESY, C.E. With above 3,000 Woodcuts. 8vo. 42s.

The Artisan Club's Treatise on the Steam Engine, in its various Applications to Mines, Mills, Steam Navigation, Railways, and Agriculture. By J. BOURNE, E.C. New Edition; with Portrait, 37 Plates, and 546 Woodcuts. 4to. 42s.

A Treatise on the Screw Propeller, Screw Vessels, and Screw Engines, as adapted for purposes of Peace and War; with notices of other Methods of Propulsion, Tables of the Dimensions and Performance of Screw Steamers, and Detailed Specifications of Ships and Engines. By the same Author. Third Edition, with 54 Plates and 287 Woodcuts. Quarto, 63s.

Catechism of the Steam Engine, in its various Applications to Mines, Mills, Steam Navigation, Railways, and Agriculture. By JOHN BOURNE, C.E. New Edition, with 89 Woodcuts. Fcp. 6s.

Handbook of the Steam Engine. By JOHN BOURNE, C.E. forming a KEY to the Author's Catechism of the Steam Engine. With 67 Woodcuts. Fcp. 9s.

Examples of Modern Steam, Air, and Gas Engines of the most Approved Types, as employed for Pumping, for Driving Machinery, for Locomotion, and for Agriculture, minutely and practically described. Illustrated by Working Drawings, and embodying a Critical Account of all Projects of Recent Improvement in Furnaces, Boilers, and Engines. By the same Author. In course of publication. Monthly, to be completed in Twenty-four Parts, price 2s. 6d. each, forming One Volume, with about 50 Plates and 400 Woodcuts.

A History of the Machine-Wrought Hosiery and Lace Manufactures. By WILLIAM FELKIN, F.L.S. F.S.S. With 3 Steel Plates, 10 Lithographic Plates of Machinery, and 10 Coloured Impressions of Patterns of Lace. Royal 8vo. 21s.

Mitchell's Manual of Practical Assaying. Third Edition, for the most part re-written, with all the recent Discoveries incorporated. By W. CROOKES, F.R.S. With 188 Woodcuts. 8vo. 28s.

Reimann's Handbook of Aniline and its Derivatives; a Treatise on the Manufacture of Aniline and Aniline Colours. Revised and edited by WILLIAM CROOKES, F.R.S. 8vo. with 5 Woodcuts, 10s. 6d.

Practical Treatise on Metallurgy, adapted from the last German Edition of Professor KERL'S *Metallurgy* by W. CROOKES, F.R.S. &c. and E. RÖHRIG, Ph.D. M.E. VOL. I. comprising *Lead, Silver, Zinc, Cadmium, Tin, Mercury, Bismuth, Antimony, Nickel, Arsenic, Gold, Platinum,* and *Sulphur.* 8vo. with 207 Woodcuts, price 31s. 6d.

The Art of Perfumery; the History and Theory of Odours, and the Methods of Extracting the Aromas of Plants. By Dr. PIESSE, F.C.S. Third Edition, with 53 Woodcuts. Crown 8vo. 10s. 6d.

Chemical, Natural, and Physical Magic, for Juveniles during the Holidays. By the same Author. Third Edition, enlarged with 38 Woodcuts. Fcp. 6s.

Loudon's Encyclopædia of Agriculture: comprising the Laying-out, Improvement, and Management of Landed Property, and the Cultivation and Economy of the Productions of Agriculture. With 1,100 Woodcuts. 8vo. 31s. 6d.

Loudon's Encyclopædia of Gardening: comprising the Theory and Practice of Horticulture, Floriculture, Arboriculture, and Landscape Gardening. With 1,000 Woodcuts. 8vo. 31s. 6d.

Bayldon's Art of Valuing Rents and Tillages, and Claims of Tenants upon Quitting Farms, both at Michaelmas and Lady-Day. Eighth Edition, revised by J. C. MORTON. 8vo. 10s. 6d.

Religious and Moral Works.

An Exposition of the 39 Articles, Historical and Doctrinal. By E. HAROLD BROWNE, D.D. Lord Bishop of Ely. Eighth Edition. 8vo. 16s.

Examination-Questions on Bishop Browne's Exposition of the Articles. By the Rev. J. GORLE, M.A. Fcp. 3s. 6d.

Archbishop Leighton's Sermons and Charges. With Additions and Corrections from MSS. and with Historical and other Illustrative Notes by WILLIAM WEST, Incumbent of S. Columba's, Nairn. 8vo. price 15s.

The Acts of the Apostles; with a Commentary, and Practical and Devotional Suggestions for Readers and Students of the English Bible. By the Rev. F. C. COOK, M.A. Canon of Exeter, &c. New Edition, 8vo. 12s. 6d.

The Life and Epistles of St. Paul. By W. J. CONYBEARE, M.A. late Fellow of Trin. Coll. Cantab. and J. S. HOWSON, D.D. Principal of Liverpool Coll.

LIBRARY EDITION, with all the Original Illustrations, Maps, Landscapes on Steel, Woodcuts, &c. 2 vols. 4to. 48s.

INTERMEDIATE EDITION, with a Selection of Maps, Plates, and Woodcuts. 2 vols. square crown 8vo. 31s. 6d.

PEOPLE'S EDITION, revised and condensed, with 46 Illustrations and Maps. 2 vols. crown 8vo. 12s.

The Voyage and Shipwreck of St. Paul; with Dissertations on the Ships and Navigation of the Ancients. By JAMES SMITH, F.R.S.. Crown 8vo. Charts, 10s. 6d.

The National Church; History and Principles of the Church Polity of England. By D. MOUNTFIELD, M.A. Rector of Newport, Salop. Crown 8vo. 4s.

Evidence of the Truth of the Christian Religion derived from the Literal Fulfilment of Prophecy, particularly as Illustrated by the History of the Jews, and the Discoveries of Recent Travellers. By ALEXANDER KEITH, D.D. 37th Edition, with numerous Plates, in square 8vo. 12s. 6d.; also the 39th Edition, in post 8vo. with 5 Plates, 6s.

The History and Destiny of the World and of the Church, according to Scripture. By the same Author. Square 8vo. with 40 Illustrations, 10s.

Ewald's History of Israel to the Death of Moses. Translated from the German. Edited, with a Preface and an Appendix, by RUSSELL MARTINEAU, M.A. Professor of Hebrew in Manchester New College, London. Second Edition, continued to the Commencement of the Monarchy. 2 vols. 8vo. 24s. VOL. II. comprising *Joshua* and *Judges*, for Purchasers of the First Edition, price 9s.

The Woman Blessed by All Generations; or, Mary the Object of Veneration, Confidence, and Imitation to all Christians. By the Rev. R. MELIA, D.D. P.S.M. With 78 Illustrations. 8vo. 15s.

Life of the Blessed Virgin: The Femall Glory. By ANTHONY STAFFORD. Together with the Apology of the Author, and an Essay on the Cultus of the Blessed Virgin Mary. Fourth Edition, with Facsimiles of the 5 Original Illustrations. Edited by the Rev. ORBY SHIPLEY, M.A. Fcp. 8vo. 10s. 6d.

Celebrated Sanctuaries of the Madonna. By the Rev. J. SPENCER NORTHCOTE, D.D. Post 8vo. 6s. 6d.

A Critical and Grammatical Com- mentary on St. Paul's Epistles. By C. J. ELLICOTT, D.D. Lord Bishop of Gloucester and Bristol. 8vo.

Galatians, Fourth Edition, 8s. 6d.
Ephesians, Fourth Edition, 8s. 6d.
Pastoral Epistles, Fourth Edition, 10s. 6d.
Philippians, Colossians, and Philemon, Third Edition, 10s. 6d.
Thessalonians, Third Edition, 7s. 6d.

An Introduction to the Study of the New Testament, Critical, Exegetical, and Theological. By the Rev. S. DAVIDSON, D.D. LL.D. 2 vols. 8vo. 30s.

Historical Lectures on the Life of Our Lord Jesus Christ: being the Hulsean Lectures for 1859. By C. J. ELLICOTT, D.D. Lord Bishop of Gloucester and Bristol. Fourth Edition. 8vo. 10s. 6d.

The Destiny of the Creature; and other Sermons preached before the University of Cambridge. By the same. Post 8vo. 5s.

The Greek Testament; with Notes, Grammatical and Exegetical. By the Rev. W. WEBSTER, M.A. and the Rev. W. F. WILKINSON, M.A. 2 vols. 8vo. £2 4s.
VOL. I. the Gospels and Acts, 20s.
VOL. II. the Epistles and Apocalypse, 24s.

Rev. T. H. Horne's Introduction to the Critical Study and Knowledge of the Holy Scriptures. Twelfth Edition, as last revised throughout and brought up to the existing State of Biblical Knowledge; under careful editorial revision. With 4 Maps and 22 Woodcuts and Facsimiles. 4 vols. 8vo. 42s.

Rev. T. H. Horne's Compendious In- troduction to the Study of the Bible, being an Analysis of the larger work by the same Author. Re-edited by the Rev. JOHN AYRE, M.A. With Maps, &c. Post 8vo. 6s.

The Treasury of Bible Know- ledge; being a Dictionary of the Books, Persons, Places, Events, and other Matters of which mention is made in Holy Scripture; Intended to establish its Authority and illustrate its Contents. By Rev. J. AYRE, M.A. With Maps, 15 Plates, and numerous Woodcuts. Fcp. 10s. 6d.

The Churchman's Daily Remem- brancer of Doctrine and Duty: consisting of Meditations taken from the Writings of Standard Divines from the Early Days of Christianity to the Present Time; with a Preface by W. R. FREMANTLE, M.A. New Edition. Fcp. 8vo. 6s.

Every-day Scripture Difficulties explained and illustrated. By J. E. PRESCOTT, M.A. VOL. I. *Matthew* and *Mark*; VOL. II. *Luke* and *John*. 2 vols. 8vo. price 9s. each.

The Pentateuch and Book of Joshua Critically Examined. By the Right Rev. J. W. COLENSO, D.D. Lord Bishop of Natal. Crown 8vo. price 6s.

The Church and the World; Three Series of Essays on Questions of the Day, by various Writers. Edited by the Rev. ORBY SHIPLEY, M.A. FIRST SERIES, Third Edition, 15s. SECOND SERIES, Second Edition, 15s. THIRD SERIES, 1868, recently published, 15s. 3 vols. 8vo. price 45s.

The Formation of Christendom. By T. W. ALLIES. PARTS I. and II. 8vo. price 12s. each.

Christendom's Divisions; a Philosophical Sketch of the Divisions of the Christian Family in East and West. By EDMUND S. FFOULKES, formerly Fellow and Tutor of Jesus Coll. Oxford. Post 8vo. 7s. 6d.

Christendom's Divisions, Part II. *Greeks and Latins*, being a History of their Dissentions and Overtures for Peace down to the Reformation. By the same Author. Post 8vo. 15s.

The Hidden Wisdom of Christ and the Key of Knowledge; or, History of the Apocrypha. By ERNEST DE BUNSEN. 2 vols. 8vo. 28s.

The Keys of St. Peter; or, the House of Rechab, connected with the History of Symbolism and Idolatry. By the same Author. 8vo. 14s.

The Power of the Soul over the Body. By GEO. MOORE, M.D. M.R.C.P.L. &c. Sixth Edition. Crown 8vo. 8s. 6d.

The Types of Genesis briefly considered as Revealing the Development of Human Nature. By ANDREW JUKES. Second Edition. Crown 8vo. 7s. 6d.

The Second Death and the Restitution of All Things, with some Preliminary Remarks on the Nature and Inspiration of Holy Scripture. By the same Author. Second Edition. Crown 8vo. 3s. 6d.

Essays and Reviews. By the Rev. W. TEMPLE, D.D. the Rev. R. WILLIAMS, B.D. the Rev. B. POWELL, M.A. the Rev. H. B. WILSON, B.D. C. W. GOODWIN, M.A. the Rev. M. PATTISON, B.D. and the Rev. B. JOWETT, M.A. 12th Edition. Fcp. 5s.

Religious Republics; Six Essays on Congregationalism. By W. M. FAWCETT, T.M. HERBERT, M.A. E. G. HERBERT, LL.B. T. H. PATTISON, P. H. PYE-SMITH, M.D. B.A. and J. ANSTIE, B.A. 8vo. price 8s. 6d.

Passing Thoughts on Religion. By the Author of 'Amy Herbert.' New Edition. Fcp. 5s.

Self-examination before Confirmation. By the same Author. 32mo. 1s. 6d.

Readings for a Month Preparatory to Confirmation from Writers of the Early and English Church. By the same. Fcp. 4s.

Readings for Every Day in Lent, compiled from the Writings of Bishop JEREMY TAYLOR. By the same. Fcp. 5s.

Preparation for the Holy Communion; the Devotions chiefly from the works of JEREMY TAYLOR. By the same. 32mo. 3s.

Bishop Jeremy Taylor's Entire Works: with Life by BISHOP HEBER. Revised and corrected by the Rev. C. P. EDEN. 10 vols. £5 5s.

England and Christendom. By ARCHBISHOP MANNING, D.D. Post 8vo. price 10s. 6d.

Principles of Education drawn from Nature and Revelation, and Applied to Female Education in the Upper Classes. By the same. 2 vols. fcp. 12s. 6d.

The Wife's Manual; or, Prayers, Thoughts, and Songs on Several Occasions of a Matron's Life. By the Rev. W. CALVERT, M.A. Crown 8vo. 10s. 6d.

Singers and Songs of the Church: being Biographical Sketches of the Hymn-Writers in all the principal Collections; with Notes on their Psalms and Hymns. By JOSIAH MILLER, M.A. New Edition, enlarged. Crown 8vo. [*Nearly ready.*

Lyra Domestica; Christian Songs for Domestic Edification. Translated from the *Psaltery and Harp* of C. J. P. SPITTA, and from other sources, by RICHARD MASSIE. FIRST and SECOND SERIES, fcp. 4s. 6d. each.

'Spiritual Songs' for the Sundays and Holidays throughout the Year. By J. S. B. MONSELL, LL.D. Vicar of Egham and Rural Dean. Fourth Edition, Sixth Thousand. Fcp. price 4s. 6d.

The Beatitudes: Abasement before God; Sorrow for Sin; Meekness of Spirit; Desire for Holiness; Gentleness; Purity of Heart; the Peace-makers; Sufferings for Christ. By the same Author. Third Edition, revised. Fcp. 3s. 6d.

His Presence not his Memory, 1855. By the same Author, in memory of his SON. Sixth Edition. 16mo. 1s.

Lyra Germanica, translated from the German by Miss C. WINKWORTH. FIRST SERIES, Hymns for the Sundays and Chief Festivals; SECOND SERIES, the Christian Life. Fcp. 3s. 6d. each SERIES.

Lyra Eucharistica; Hymns and Verses on the Holy Communion, Ancient and Modern: with other Poems. Edited by the Rev. ORBY SHIPLEY, M.A. Second Edition. Fcp. 7s. 6d.

By the same Editor,
Lyra Messianica. Fcp. 7s. 6d.
Lyra Mystica. Fcp. 7s. 6d.

16　　　　NEW WORKS PUBLISHED BY LONGMANS AND CO.

Palm Leaves: Sacred Poems selected and translated from the German of KARL GEROK. By CATHERINE WINKWORTH.
[*In the press.*

Endeavours after the Christian Life: Discourses. By JAMES MARTINEAU. Fourth and Cheaper Edition, carefully revised; the Two Series complete in One Volume. Post 8vo. 7s. 6d.

Invocation of Saints; a Journal of Devotions for the use of Members of the English Church. Edited by the Rev. ORBY SHIPLEY, M.A. [*In the press.*

Introductory Lessons on the History of Religious Worship; being a Sequel to the same Author's 'Lessons on Christian Evidences.' By RICHARD WHATELY, D.D. New Edition. 18mo. 2s. 6d.

Travels, Voyages, &c.

Six Months in India. By MARY CARPENTER. 2 vols. post 8vo. with Portrait, 18s.

Letters from Australia, comprising the Voyage Outwards, Melbourne, Ballarat, Squatting in Victoria, Tasmania, Sydney, &c. By JOHN MARTINEAU. [*Nearly ready.*

Cadore or Titian's Country. By JOSIAH GILBERT, one of the Authors of the 'Dolomite Mountains, or Excursions through Tyrol, Carinthia, Carniola, and Friuli.' In One Volume with numerous Illustrations and a Facsimile of Titian's Original Design for his Picture of the Battle of Cadore.
[*Nearly ready.*

The Dolomite Mountains. Excursions through Tyrol, Carinthia, Carniola, and Friuli. By J. GILBERT and G. C. CHURCHILL, F.R.G.S. With numerous Illustrations. Square crown 8vo. 21s.

Pictures in Tyrol and Elsewhere. From a Family Sketch-Book. By the Author of 'A Voyage en Zigzag,' &c. Second Edition. 4to. with many Illustrations, 21s.

How we Spent the Summer; or, a Voyage en Zigzag in Switzerland and Tyrol with some Members of the ALPINE CLUB. From the Sketch-Book of one of the Party. Third Edition, re-drawn. In oblong 4to. with about 300 Illustrations, 15s.

Beaten Tracks; or, Pen and Pencil Sketches in Italy. By the Authoress of 'A Voyage en Zigzag.' With 42 Plates, containing about 200 Sketches from Drawings made on the Spot. 8vo. 16s.

Map of the Chain of Mont Blanc, from an actual Survey in 1863—1864. By A. ADAMS-REILLY, F.R.G.S. M.A.C. Published under the Authority of the Alpine Club. In Chromolithography on extra stout drawing paper 28in. × 17in. price 10s. or mounted on canvas in a folding case, 12s. 6d.

History of Discovery in our Australasian Colonies, Australia, Tasmania, and New Zealand, from the Earliest Date to the Present Day. By WILLIAM HOWITT. With 3 Maps of the Recent Explorations from Official Sources. 2 vols. 8vo. 20s.

The Capital of the Tycoon; a Narrative of a 3 Years' Residence in Japan. By Sir RUTHERFORD ALCOCK, K.C.B. 2 vols. 8vo. with numerous Illustrations, 42s.

The North-West Peninsula of Iceland; being the Journal of a Tour in Iceland in the Summer of 1862. By C. W. SHEPHERD, M.A. F.Z.S. With a Map and Two Illustrations. Fcp. 8vo. 7s. 6d.

Guide to the Pyrenees, for the use of Mountaineers. By CHARLES PACKE. Second Edition, with Maps, &c. and Appendix. Crown 8vo. 7s 6d.

The Alpine Guide. By JOHN BALL, M.R.I.A. late President of the Alpine Club. Post 8vo. with Maps and other Illustrations.

Guide to the Eastern Alps, price 10s. 6d.

Guide to the Western Alps, including Mont Blanc, Monte Rosa, Zermatt, &c. price 6s. 6d.

Guide to the Central Alps, including all the Oberland District, price 7s. 6d.

Introduction on Alpine Travelling in general, and on the Geology of the Alps, price 1s. Either of the Three Volumes or Parts of the *Alpine Guide* may be had with this INTRODUCTION prefixed, price 1s. extra

Roma Sotterranea; or, an Account of the Roman Catacombs, and especially of the Cemetery of St. Callixtus. Compiled from the Works of Commendatore G. B. DE ROSSI, with the consent of the Author, by the Rev. J. S. NORTHCOTE, D.D. and the Rev. W. B. BROWNLOW. With numerous Engravings on Wood, 10 Lithographs, 10 Plates in Chromolithography, and an Atlas of Plans, all executed in Rome under the Author's superintendence for this Translation. 1 vol. 8vo. [*Nearly ready.*

The Irish in America. By JOHN FRANCIS MAGUIRE, M.P. for Cork. Post 8vo. 12s. 6d.

Memorials of London and London Life in the 13th, 14th, and 15th Centuries; being a Series of Extracts, Local, Social, and Political, from the Archives of the City of London, A.D. 1276-1419. Selected, translated, and edited by H. T. RILEY, M.A. Royal 8vo. 21s.

Commentaries on the History, Constitution, and Chartered Franchises of the City of London. By GEORGE NORTON, formerly one of the Common Pleaders of the City of London. Third Edition. 8vo. 14s.

Curiosities of London; exhibiting the most Rare and Remarkable Objects of Interest in the Metropolis; with nearly Sixty Years' Personal Recollections. By JOHN TIMBS, F.S.A. New Edition, corrected and enlarged. 8vo. Portrait, 21s.

The Northern Heights of London; or, Historical Associations of Hampstead, Highgate, Muswell Hill, Hornsey, and Islington. By WILLIAM HOWITT. With about 40 Woodcuts. Square crown 8vo. 21s.

The Rural Life of England. By the same Author. With Woodcuts by Bewick and Williams. Medium, 8vo. 12s. 6d.

Visits to Remarkable Places: Old Halls, Battle-Fields, and Scenes illustrative of striking Passages in English History and Poetry. By the same Author. 2 vols. square crown 8vo. with Wood Engravings, 25s.

Narratives of Shipwrecks of the Royal Navy between 1793 and 1857, compiled from Official Documents in the Admiralty by W. O. S. GILLY; with a Preface by W. S. GILLY, D.D. 3rd Edition, fcp. 5s.

Narrative of the Euphrates Expedition carried on by Order of the British Government during the years 1835, 1836, and 1837. By General F. R. CHESNEY, F.R.S. With 2 Maps, 45 Plates, and 16 Woodcuts. 8vo. 24s.

Travels in Abyssinia and the Galla Country; with an Account of a Mission to Ras Ali in 1848. From the MSS. of the late W. C. PLOWDEN, H. B. M. Consul in Abyssinia. Edited by his Brother T. C. PLOWDEN. 8vo. with Maps, 18s.

Works of Fiction.

The Warden; a Novel. By ANTHONY TROLLOPE. Crown 8vo. 2s. 6d.

Barchester Towers; a Sequel to 'The Warden.' Crown 8vo. 3s. 6d.

Stories and Tales by the Author of 'Amy Herbert,' uniform Edition, each Tale or Story a single volume:—

AMY HERBERT, 2s. 6d. | KATHARINE ASHTON, 3s. 6d.
GERTRUDE, 2s. 6d. |
EARL'S DAUGHTER, 2s. 6d. | MARGARET PERCIVAL, 5s.
EXPERIENCE OF LIFE, 2s. 6d. | LANETON PARSONAGE, 4s. 6d.
CLEVE HALL, 3s. 6d. | URSULA, 4s. 6d.
IVORS, 3s. 6d. |

A Glimpse of the World. Fcp. 7s. 6d.

Journal of a Home Life. Post 8vo. 9s. 6d.

After Life; a Sequel to the 'Journal of a Home Life.' Post 8vo. 10s 6d.

Uncle Peter's Fairy Tale for the XIXth Century. Edited by ELIZABETH M. SEWELL, Author of 'Amy Herbert,' &c. Fcp. 8vo. 7s. 6d.

Becker's Gallus; or, Roman Scenes of the Time of Augustus. Post 8vo. 7s. 6d.

Becker's Charicles: Illustrative of Private Life of the Ancient Greeks. Post 8vo. 7s. 6d.

Tales of Ancient Greece. By GEORGE W. Cox, M.A. late Scholar of Trin. Coll. Oxford. Being a collective Edition of the Author's Classical Series and Tales, complete in One Volume. Crown 8vo. 6s. 6d.

A Manual of Mythology, in the form of Question and Answer. By the Rev. GEORGE W. Cox, M.A. late Scholar of Trinity College, Oxford. Fcp. 3s.

Cabinet Edition of Novels and Tales by J. G. WHYTE MELVILLE:—

THE GLADIATORS, 5s. | HOLMBY HOUSE, 5s.
DIGBY GRAND, 5s. | GOOD FOR NOTHING 6s.
KATE COVENTRY, 5s. | QUEEN'S MARIES, 6s.
GENERAL BOUNCE, 5s | THE INTERPRETER, 5s.

Poetry and The Drama.

Thomas Moore's Poetical Works, the only Editions containing the Author's last Copyright Additions:—
Shamrock Edition, price 3s. 6d.
Ruby Edition, with Portrait, 6s.
People's Edition, Portrait, &c. 12s. 6d.
Library Edition, Portrait & Vignette, 14s.
Cabinet Edition, 10 vols. fcp. 8vo. 35s.

Moore's Lalla Rookh, Tenniel's Edition, with 68 Wood Engravings from Original Drawings and other Illustrations. Fcp. 4to. 21s.

Moore's Irish Melodies, Maclise's Edition, with 161 Steel Plates from Original Drawings. Super-royal 8vo. 31s. 6d.

Miniature Edition of Moore's Irish Melodies, with Maclise's Illustrations (as above), reduced in Lithography. Imp. 16mo. 10s. 6d.

Southey's Poetical Works, with the Author's last Corrections and copywright Additions. Library Edition. In 1 vol. medium 8vo. with Portrait and Vignette, 14s. or in 10 vols. fcp. 3s. 6d. each.

Lays of Ancient Rome; with Ivry and the Armada. By the Right Hon. LORD MACAULAY. 16mo. 4s. 6d.

Lord Macaulay's Lays of Ancient Rome. With 90 Illustrations on Wood, Original and from the Antique, from Drawings by G. SCHARF. Fcp. 4to. 21s.

Miniature Edition of Lord Macaulay's Lays of Ancient Rome, with Scharf's Illustrations (as above) reduced in Lithography. Imp. 16mo. 10s. 6d.

Goldsmith's Poetical Works, Illustrated with Wood Engravings from Designs by Members of the ETCHING CLUB. Imp. 16mo. 7s. 6d.

Poems. By JEAN INGELOW. Twelfth Edition. Fcp. 8vo. 5s.

Poems by Jean Ingelow. A New Edition, with nearly 100 Illustrations by Eminent Artists, engraved on Wood by the Brothers DALZIEL. Fcp. 4to. 21s.

A Story of Doom, and other Poems. By JEAN INGELOW. Fcp. 5s.

Poetical Works of Letitia Elizabeth Landon (L.E.L.) 2 vols. 16mo. 10s.

Playtime with the Poets: a Selection of the best English Poetry, for the use of Children. By a LADY. Crown 8vo. 5s.

Memories of some Contemporary Poets; with Selections from their Writings. By EMILY TAYLOR. Royal 18mo. 5s.

Bowdler's Family Shakspeare, cheaper Genuine Edition, complete in 1 vol. large type, with 36 Woodcut Illustrations, price 14s. or in 6 pocket vols. 3s. 6d. each.

Arundines Cami, sive Musarum Cantabrigiensium Lusus Canori. Collegit atque edidit H. DRURY, M.A. Editio Sexta, curavit H. J. HODGSON, M.A. Crown 8vo. price 7s. 6d.

Horatii Opera, Pocket Edition, with carefully corrected Text, Marginal References, and Introduction. Edited by the Rev. J. E. YONGE, M.A. Square 18mo. 4s. 6d.

Horatii Opera, Library Edition, with Copious English Notes, Marginal References and Various Readings. Edited by the Rev. J. E. YONGE, M.A. 8vo. 21s.

Eight Comedies of Aristophanes, viz. the Acharnians, Knights, Clouds, Wasps, Peace, Birds, Frogs, and Plutus. Translated into Rhymed Metres by LEONARD-HAMPSON RUDD, M.A. 8vo. 15s.

The Æneid of Virgil Translated into English Verse. By JOHN CONINGTON, M.A. Corpus Professor of Latin in the University of Oxford. Crown 8vo. 9s.

The Iliad of Homer Translated into Blank Verse. By ICHABOD CHARLES WRIGHT, M.A. 2 vols. crown 8vo. 21s.

The Iliad of Homer in English Hexameter Verse. By J. HENRY DART, M.A. of Exeter College, Oxford. Square crown 8vo. 21s.

The Odyssey of Homer. Translated into Blank Verse by G. W. EDGINTON, Licentiate in Medicine. Dedicated by permission to Edward Earl of Derby. VOL. I. 8vo. with Map, 10s. 6d.

Dante's Divine Comedy, translated in English Terza Rima by JOHN DAYMAN, M.A. [With the Italian Text, after Brunetti, interpaged.] 8vo. 21s.

The Holy Child. A Poem in Four Cantos; also an Ode to Silence, and other Poems. By S. JENNER, M.A. Fcp. 8vo. 5s.

French Poetry, with English Notes for Students. By the late Professor VENTOUILLAC. Eighth Edition. 18mo. 2s.

The Three Fountains, a Faëry Epic of Euboea; with other Verses. By the Author of 'The Afterglow.' Fcp. 3s. 6d.

The Afterglow; Songs and Sonnets for my Friends. By the Author of 'The Three Fountains.' Second Edition. Fcp. 8vo. 5s.

An Old Story, and other Poems. By ELIZABETH D. CROSS. Second Edition. Fcp. 8vo. 3s. 6d.

Hunting Songs and Miscellaneous Verses. By R. E. EGERTON WARBURTON. Second Edition. Fcp. 8vo. 5s.

Rural Sports, &c.

Encyclopædia of Rural Sports; a Complete Account, Historical, Practical, and Descriptive, of Hunting, Shooting, Fishing, Racing, &c. By D. P. BLAINE. With above 600 Woodcuts (20 from Designs by JOHN LEECH). 8vo. 42s.

Col. Hawker's Instructions to Young Sportsmen in all that relates to Guns and Shooting. Revised by the Author's SON. Square crown 8vo. with Illustrations, 18s.

The Dead Shot, or Sportsman's Complete Guide; a Treatise on the Use of the Gun, Dog-breaking, Pigeon-shooting, &c. By MARKSMAN. Fcp. with Plates, 5s.

A Book on Angling: being a Complete Treatise on the Art of Angling in every branch, including full Illustrated Lists of Salmon Flies. By FRANCIS FRANCIS, Second Edition, with Portrait and 15 other Plates, plain and coloured. Post 8vo. 15s.

Wilcocks's Sea-Fisherman: comprising the Chief Methods of Hook and Line Fishing in the British and other Seas, a glance at Nets, and remarks on Boats and Boating. Second Edition, enlarged, with 80 Woodcuts. Post 8vo. 12s. 6d.

The Fly-Fisher's Entomology. By ALFRED RONALDS. With coloured Representations of the Natural and Artificial Insect. Sixth Edition, with 20 coloured Plates. 8vo. 14s.

Blaine's Veterinary Art: a Treatise on the Anatomy, Physiology, and Curative Treatment of the Diseases of the Horse, Neat Cattle, and Sheep. Seventh Edition, revised and enlarged by C. STEEL. 8vo. with Plates and Woodcuts, 18s.

The Cricket Field; or, the History and the Science of the Game of Cricket. By JAMES PYCROFT, B.A. 4th Edition, fcp. 5s.

Horse and Man. By C. S. MARCH PHILLIPPS, Author of 'Jurisprudence,' &c. Fcp. 8vo. 2s. 6d.

Youatt on the Horse. Revised and enlarged by W. WATSON, M.R.C.V.S. 8vo. with numerous Woodcuts, 12s. 6d.

Youatt on the Dog. (By the same Author.) 8vo. with numerous Woodcuts, 6s.

The Horse's Foot, and how to keep it Sound. By W. MILES, Esq. Ninth Edition, with Illustrations. Imp. 8vo. 12s. 6d.

A Plain Treatise on Horse-shoeing. By the same Author. Sixth Edition, post 8vo. with Illustrations, 2s. 6d.

Stables and Stable Fittings. By the same. Imp. 8vo. with 13 Plates, 15s.

Remarks on Horses' Teeth, addressed to Purchasers. By the same. Post 8vo. 1s. 6d.

Robbins's Cavalry Catechism; or, Instructions on Cavalry Exercise and Field Movements, Brigade Movements, Out-post Duty, Cavalry supporting Artillery, Artillery attached to Cavalry. 12mo. 5s.

The Dog in Health and Disease. By STONEHENGE. With 70 Wood Engravings. New Edition. Square crown 8vo. 10s. 6d.

The Greyhound. By the same Author. Revised Edition, with 24 Portraits of Greyhounds. Square crown 8vo. 10s. 6d.

The Ox, his Diseases and their Treatment; with an Essay on Parturition in the Cow. By J. R. DOBSON, M.R.C.V.S. Crown 8vo. with Illustrations, 7s. 6d.

Commerce, Navigation, and Mercantile Affairs.

Banking, Currency, and the Exchanges: a Practical Treatise. By ARTHUR CRUMP, Bank Manager, formerly of the Bank of England. Post 8vo. 6s.

The Theory and Practice of Banking. By HENRY DUNNING MACLEOD, M.A. Barrister-at-Law. Second Edition entirely remodelled. 2 vols. 8vo. 30s.

The Elements of Banking. By HENRY DUNNING MACLEOD, M.A. of Trinity College, Cambridge, and of the Inner Temple, Barrister-at-Law. Post 8vo. [*Nearly ready.*

The Law of Nations Considered as Independent Political Communities. By Sir TRAVERS TWISS, D.C.L. 2 vols. 8vo. 30s. or separately, PART I *Peace*, 12s. PART II. *War*, 18s.

M'Culloch's Dictionary, Practical, Theoretical, and Historical, of Commerce and Commercial Navigation. New Edition, revised throughout and corrected to the Present Time. 8vo. price 63s. cloth, or 70s. half-bound in russia.

Practical Guide for British Shipmasters to United States Ports. By PIERREPONT EDWARDS, Her Britannic Majesty's Vice-Consul at New York. Post 8vo. 8s. 6d.

Works of Utility and General Information.

Modern Cookery for Private Families, reduced to a System of Easy Practice in a Series of carefully-tested Receipts. By ELIZA ACTON. Newly revised and enlarged; with 8 Plates, Figures, and 150 Woodcuts. Fcp. 6s.

On Food and its Digestion; an Introduction to Dietetics. By W. BRINTON, M.D. Physician to St. Thomas's Hospital, &c. With 48 Woodcuts. Post 8vo. 12s.

Wine, the Vine, and the Cellar. By THOMAS G. SHAW. Second Edition, revised and enlarged, with Frontispiece and 31 Illustrations on Wood. 8vo. 16s.

A Practical Treatise on Brewing; with Formulæ for Public Brewers, and Instructions for Private Families. By W. BLACK. Fifth Edition. 8vo. 10s. 6d.

Short Whist. By MAJOR A. A thoroughly revised Edition; with an Essay on the Theory of the Modern Scientific Game by Professor P. Fcp. 8vo. 3s. 6d.

Whist, What to Lead. By CAM. Third Edition. 32mo. 1s.

The Cabinet Lawyer; a Popular Digest of the Laws of England, Civil, Criminal, and Constitutional. 24th Edition; with Supplements of the Acts of the Parliamentary Sessions of 1867 and 1868. Fcp. 10s. 6d.

The Philosophy of Health; or, an Exposition of the Physiological and Sanitary Conditions conducive to Human Longevity and Happiness. By SOUTHWOOD SMITH, M.D. Eleventh Edition, revised and enlarged; with 113 Woodcuts. 8vo. 7s. 6d.

A Handbook for Readers at the British Museum. By THOMAS NICHOLS. Post 8vo. 6s.

Maunder's Treasury of Knowledge and Library of Reference: comprising an English Dictionary and Grammar, Universal Gazetteer, Classical Dictionary, Chronology, Law Dictionary, Synopsis of the Peerage, Useful Tables, &c. Fcp. 10s. 6d.

Hints to Mothers on the Management of their Health during the Period of Pregnancy and in the Lying-in Room. By T. BULL, M.D. Fcp. 5s.

The Maternal Management of Children in Health and Disease. By the same Author. Fcp. 5s.

How to Nurse Sick Children; containing Directions which may be found of service to all who have charge of the Young. By CHARLES WEST, M.D. Second Edition. Fcp. 8vo. 2s. 6d.

Notes on Hospitals. By FLORENCE NIGHTINGALE. Third Edition, enlarged; with 13 Plans. Post 4to. 18s.

Instructions in Household Matters; or, the Young Girl's Guide to Domestic Service. Written by a LADY for the use of Girls intended for Service on leaving School. Seventh Edition. Fcp. 1s. 6d.

Mary's Every-Day Book of useful and Miscellaneous Knowledge; illustrated with Stories, and intended for the use of Children. By FRANCES E. BURBURY, Author of 'Mary's Geography.' 18mo. 3s. 6d.

The Law relating to Benefit Building Societies; with Practical Observations on the Act and all the Cases decided thereon, also a Form of Rules and Forms of Mortgages. By W. TIDD PRATT, Barrister. 2nd Edition. Fcp. 3s. 6d.

Willich's Popular Tables for Ascertaining the Value of Lifehold, Leasehold, and Church Property, Renewal Fines, &c.; the Public Funds; Annual Average Price and Interest on Consols from 1731 to 1867; Chemical, Geographical, Astronomical, Trigonometrical Tables, &c. Post 8vo. 10s.

Decimal Interest Tables at Twenty-four Different Rates not exceeding Five per Cent. Calculated for the use of Bankers. To which are added Commission Tables at One-eighth and One-fourth per Cent. By J. R. COULTHART. New Edition. 8vo. 15s.

INDEX.

Acton's Modern Cookery	20
Afterglow (The)	19
Alcock's Residence in Japan	16
Allies on Formation of Christianity	15
Alpine Guide (The)	16
Apjohn's Manual of the Metalloids	9
Arnold's Manual of English Literature	5
Arnott's Elements of Physics	8
Arundines Cami	18
Autumn Holidays of a Country Parson	6
Ayre's Treasury of Bible Knowledge	14
Bacon's Essays by Whately	5
——— Life and Letters, by Spedding	3
——— Works	4
Bain's Mental and Moral Science	7
——— on the Emotions and Will	7
——— on the Senses and Intellect	7
——— on the Study of Character	7
Ball's Guide to the Central Alps	16
———Guide to the Western Alps	16
———Guide to the Eastern Alps	16
Barnard's Drawing from Nature	12
Bayldon's Rents and Tillages	13
Beaten Tracks	16
Becker's *Charicles* and *Gallus*	17
Benfey's Sanskrit-English Dictionary	6
Black's Treatise on Brewing	20
Blackley's Word-Gossip	7
Blackley and Friedländer's German and English Dictionary	6
Blaine's Rural Sports	10
——— Veterinary Art	19
Booth's Epigrams	6
Bourne on Screw Propeller	12
———'s Catechism of the Steam Engine	12
——— Examples of Modern Engines	13
——— Handbook of Steam Engine	13
——— Treatise on the Steam Engine	12
Bowdler's Family Shakspeare	18
Brande's Dictionary of Science, Literature, and Art	9
Bray's (C.) Education of the Feelings	7
——— Philosophy of Necessity	7
——— On Force	7
Brinton on Food and Digestion	20
Brodie's (Sir C. B.) Works	10
Browne's Exposition of the 39 Articles	13
Buckle's History of Civilisation	2
Bull's Hints to Mothers	20
——— Maternal Management of Children	20
Bunsen's Ancient Egypt	3
——— God in History	3
——— Memoirs	3
Bunsen (E. De) on Apocrypha	15
———'s Keys of St. Peter	15
Burbury's Mary's Every Day Book	20
Burke's Vicissitudes of Families	4
Burton's Christian Church	3
Cabinet Lawyer	20
Calvert's Wife's Manual	15
Cannon's Grant's Campaign	2
Carpenter's Six Months in India	16
Cates's Biographical Dictionary	3
Cats and Farlie's Moral Emblems	11
Changed Aspects of Unchanged Truths	6
Chesney's Euphrates Expedition	17
——— Indian Polity	2
——— Waterloo Campaign	2
Child's Physiological Essays	10
Chorale Book for England	11
Churchman's Daily Remembrancer	14
Clough's Lives from Plutarch	2
Cobbe's Norman Kings	3
Colenso (Bishop) on Pentateuch and Book of Joshua	14
Commonplace Philosopher in Town and Country	6
Conington's Chemical Analysis	9
——— Translation of Virgil's Æneid	18
Contanseau's Two French Dictionaries	6
Conybeare and Howson's Life and Epistles of St. Paul	13
Cook's Acts of the Apostles	13
——— Voyages	4
Copland's Dictionary of Practical Medicine	10
Coulthart's Decimal Interest Tables	20
Counsel and Comfort from a City Pulpit	6
Cox's (G. W.) Manual of Mythology	17
——— Tale of the Great Persian War	2
——— Tales of Ancient Greece	17
——— (H.) Ancient Parliamentary Elections	1
——— History of the Reform Bills	1
——— Whig and Tory Administrations	1
Cresy's Encyclopædia of Civil Engineering	12
Critical Essays of a Country Parson	6
Cross's Old Story	19
Crowe's History of France	2
Crump on Banking, &c.	19
Culley's Handbook of Telegraphy	12
Cusack's History of Ireland	2
Dart's Iliad of Homer	18
D'Aubigné's History of the Reformation in the time of Calvin	2
Davidson's Introduction to New Testament	14
Dayman's Dante's Divina Commedia	18
Dead Shot (The), by Marksman	19
De la Rive's Treatise on Electricity	8

De Tocqueville's Democracy in America	2
Dobson on the Ox	19
Dove's Law of Storms	8
Dyer's City of Rome	2
Eastlake's Hints on Household Taste	12
———— History of Oil Painting	11
Edginton's Odyssey	18
Edwards's Shipmaster's Guide	20
Elements of Botany	9
Ellicott's Commentary on Ephesians	14
———— Destiny of the Creature	14
———— Lectures on Life of Christ	14
———— Commentary on Galatians	14
———— Pastoral Epist.	14
———— Philippians,&c.	14
———— Thessalonians	14
Essays and Reviews	15
Ewald's History of Israel	14
Fairbairn's Application of Cast and Wrought Iron to Building	12
———— Information for Engineers	12
———— Treatise on Mills and Millwork	12
Fairbairn on Iron Shipbuilding	12
Farrar's Chapters on Language	5
Felkin on Hosiery & Lace Manufactures	13
Ffoulkes's Christendom's Divisions	15
Fitzgibbon's Ireland	2
Fliedner's (Pastor) Life	3
Forbes's Earls of Granard	4
Francis's Fishing Book	19
Froude's History of England	1
———— Short Studies	6
Ganot's Elementary Physics	8
Gilbert's Cadore	16
———— and Churchill's Dolomite Mountains	16
Gilly's Shipwrecks of the Navy	17
Girtin's House I Live In	10
Goldsmith's Poems, Illustrated	18
Goodeve's Elements of Mechanism	12
Gould's Silver Store	6
Graham's Book About Words	5
Grant's Ethics of Aristotle	5
Graver Thoughts of a Country Parson	6
Gray's Anatomy	10
Greene's Corals and Sea Jellies	9
———— Sponges and Animalculae	9
Greenhow on Bronchitis	10
Grove on Correlation of Physical Forces	8
Gwilt's Encyclopædia of Architecture	12
Hare on Election of Representatives	5
Hartwig's Harmonies of Nature	9
———— Polar World	9
———— Sea and its Living Wonders	9
———— Tropical World	9
Haughton's Manual of Geology	8
Hawker's Instructions to Young Sportsmen	19
Henderson's Folk-Lore	6
Herschel's Outlines of Astronomy	7
———— Preliminary Discourse on the Study of Natural Philosophy	8

Hewitt on the Diseases of Women	10
Holmes's Surgical Treatment of Children	10
———— System of Surgery	10
Hooker and Walker-Arnott's British Flora	9
Horne's Introduction to the Scriptures	14
———— Compendium of the Scriptures	14
How we Spent the Summer	16
Howard's Gymnastic Exercises	11
Howitt's Australian Discovery	16
———— Northern Heights of London	17
———— Rural Life of England	17
———— Visits to Remarkable Places	17
Hughes's Manual of Geography	7
Hullah's Lectures on Modern Music	11
———— Part Music, Sacred and Secular	11
———— Sacred Music	11
Humphreys's Sentiments of Shakspeare	11
Hutton's Studies in Parliament	6
Hymns from Lyra Germanica	14
Icelandic Legends, Second Series	17
Ingelow's Poems	18
———— Story of Doom	18
Instructions in Household Matters	20
Jameson's Legends of Saints and Martyrs	11
———— Legends of the Madonna	11
———— Legends of the Monastic Orders	11
———— Legends of the Saviour	11
Jenner's Holy Child	18
Johnston's Geographical Dictionary	7
Jordan on Vis Inertiæ in Ocean	8
Jukes on Second Death	15
———— on Types of Genesis	15
Kalisch's Commentary on the Bible	5
———— Hebrew Grammar	5
Keith on Destiny of the World	14
———— Fulfilment of Prophecy	14
Kerl's Metallurgy, by Crookes and Röhrig	13
Kesteven's Domestic Medicine	10
Kirby and Spence's Entomology	9
Landon's (L. E. L.) Poetical Works	18
Latham's English Dictionary	5
———— River Plate	7
Lecky's History of European Morals	3
———— Rationalism	3
Leighton's Sermons and Charges	13
Leisure Hours in Town	6
Lessons of Middle Age	6
Lewes's Biographical History of Philosophy	3
Liddell and Scott's Greek-English Lexicon	5
———— Abridged ditto	6
Life of Man Symbolised	11
Lindley and Moore's Treasury of Botany	9
Longman's Edward the Third	2
———— Lectures on History of England	2
Loudon's Encyclopædia of Agriculture	13
———— Gardening	13
———— Plants	9
Lowndes's Engineer's Handbook	12

LYRA Domestica	15
—— Eucharistica	15
—— Germanica	11, 15
—— Messianica	15
—— Mystica	15
MACAULAY'S (Lord) Essays	3
———————— History of England	1
———————— Lays of Ancient Rome	19
———————— Miscellaneous Writings	6
———————— Speeches	5
———————— Works	1
MACFARREN'S Lectures on Harmony	11
MACLEOD'S Elements of Political Economy	4
———— Dictionary of Political Economy	4
———— Elements of Banking	20
———— Theory and Practice of Banking	19
MCCULLOCH'S Dictionary of Commerce	19
———— Geographical Dictionary	7
MAGUIRE'S Irish in America	17
MAGUIRE'S Life of Father Mathew	3
MALLESON'S French in India	2
MANNING'S England and Christendom	15
MARSHALL'S Physiology	10
MARSHMAN'S History of India	2
———— Life of Havelock	4
MARTINEAU'S Endeavours after the Christian Life	16
MARTINEAU'S Letters from Australia	16
MASSEY'S History of England	1
MASSINGBERD'S History of the Reformation	3
MAUNDER'S Biographical Treasury	4
———— Geographical Treasury	7
———— Historical Treasury	3
———— Scientific and Literary Treasury	9
———— Treasury of Knowledge	20
———— Treasury of Natural History	9
MAURY'S Physical Geography	7
MAY'S Constitutional History of England	1
MEISSNER'S Biographical and Critical Essays	4
MELIA on Virgin Mary	14
MELVILLE'S Digby Grand	17
———— General Bounce	17
———— Gladiators	17
———— Good for Nothing	17
———— Holmby House	17
———— Interpreter	17
———— Kate Coventry	17
———— Queen's Maries	17
MENDELSSOHN'S Letters	4
MERIVALE'S (H.) Historical Studies	1
———— (C.) Fall of the Roman Republic	2
———— Romans under the Empire	2
———— Boyle Lectures	2
MERRIFIELD and EVERS'S Navigation	7
MILES on Horse's Foot and Horse Shoeing	19
———— on Horses' Teeth and Stables	19
MILL (J.) on the Mind	4
MILL (J. S.) on Liberty	4
———— on Representative Government	4
———— on Utilitarianism	4
———— 's Dissertations and Discussions	4
———— Political Economy	4
———— System of Logic	4
———— Hamilton's Philosophy	4
———— Inaugural Address at St. Andrew's	4
MILLER'S Elements of Chemistry	9
———— Hymn Writers	15
MITCHELL'S Manual of Assaying	13
Modern Ireland	2
MONSELL'S Beatitudes	15
———— His Presence not his Memory	15
———— 'Spiritual Songs'	15
MOORE'S Irish Melodies	18
———— Lalla Rookh	18
———— Journal and Correspondence	3
———— Poetical Works	18
———— (Dr. G.) First Man	8
———— Power of the Soul over the Body	15
MORELL'S Elements of Psychology	7
———— Mental Philosophy	7
MOUNTFIELD on National Church	14
MÜLLER'S (Max) Chips from a German Workshop	7
———— Lectures on the Science of Language	5
———— (K. O.) Literature of Ancient Greece	2
MURCHISON on Continued Fevers	10
———— on Liver Complaints	10
MURE'S Language and Literature of Greece	2
New Testament Illustrated with Wood Engravings from the Old Masters	11
NEWMAN'S History of his Religious Opinions	3
NICHOLAS'S Pedigree of the English People	6
NICHOLS'S Handbook to British Museum	20
NIGHTINGALE'S Notes on Hospitals	20
NILSSON'S Scandinavia	8
NORTHCOTE'S Sanctuary of the Madonna	14
NORTHCOTT on Lathes and Turning	12
NORTON'S City of London	17
ODLING'S Animal Chemistry	10
———— Course of Practical Chemistry	10
———— Manual of Chemistry	9
Original Designs for Wood Carving	12
OWEN'S Comparative Anatomy and Physiology of Vertebrate Animals	8
OWEN'S Lectures on the Invertebrata	8
PACKE'S Guide to the Pyrenees	16
PAGET'S Lectures on Surgical Pathology	10
Palm Leaves	16
PEREIRA'S Manual of Materia Medica	11
PERKINS'S Italian and Tuscan Sculptors	12
PHILLIPS'S Guide to Geology	8
PHILLIPPS'S Horse and Man	19
Pictures in Tyrol	16
PIESSE'S Art of Perfumery	13
———— Chemical, Natural, and Physical Magic	13
PIKE'S English and their Origin	6
Playtime with the Poets	18
PLOWDEN'S Abyssinia	17
POLKO'S Reminiscences of Mendelssohn	4
PRATT'S Law of Building Societies	20
PRESCOTT'S Scripture Difficulties	14
PROCTOR'S Handbook of the Stars	7
———— Saturn	7
PYCROFT'S Cricket Field	19
Quarterly Journal of Science	9
QUICK'S Educational Reformers	4

RAYMOND on Fishing without Cruelty	18
Recreations of a Country Parson	6
REILLY's Map of Mont Blanc	16
REIMANN on Aniline Dyes	13
Religious Republics	15
RICHARDSON's Life, by M'Ilwraith	4
RILEY's Memorials of London	17
RIVERS's Rose Amateur's Guide	9
ROBBINS's Cavalry Catechism	19
ROGERS's Correspondence of Greyson	7
———— Eclipse of Faith	7
———— Defence of Faith	7
———— Essays from the *Edinburgh Review*	6
———— Reason and Faith	6
ROGET's Thesaurus of English Words and Phrases	5
Roma Sotterranea	16
RONALDS's Fly-Fisher's Entomology	19
ROWTON's Debater	5
RUDD's Aristophanes	18
RUSSELL on Government and Constitution	1
SANDARS's Justinian's Institutes	5
SCHEFFLER on Ocular Defects	10
SCHUBERT's Life, translated by COLERIDGE	3
SCOTT's Lectures on the Fine Arts	11
SEEBOHM's Oxford Reformers of 1498	2
SENIOR's Journals &c. relating to Ireland	2
SEWELL's After Life	17
———— Glimpse of the World	17
———— History of the Early Church	3
———— Journal of a Home Life	17
———— Passing Thoughts on Religion	15
———— Preparation for Communion	15
———— Principles of Education	15
———— Readings for Confirmation	15
———— Readings for Lent	15
———— Examination for Confirmation	15
———— Stories and Tales	17
SHAKSPEARE's Midsummer Night's Dream, illustrated with Silhouettes	11
SHAW's Work on Wine	20
SHEPHERD's Iceland	16
SHIPLEY's Church and the World	14
———— Invocation of Saints	16
Short Whist	20
SHORT's Church History	3
Smart's WALKER's English Pronouncing Dictionaries	5
SMITH's (SOUTHWOOD) Philosophy of Health	20
———— (J.) Paul's Voyage and Shipwreck	13
———— (SYDNEY) Miscellaneous Works	6
———— Wit and Wisdom	6
SOUTHEY's (Doctor)	5
———— Poetical Works	18
STAFFORD's Life of the Blessed Virgin	14
STANLEY's History of British Birds	9
STEBBING's Analysis of MILL's Logic	4
STEPHEN's Essays in Ecclesiastical Biography	4
STIRLING's Secret of Hegel	7
STOKES's Life of Petrie	4
STONEHENGE on the Dog	19
———— on the Greyhound	19
STRICKLAND's Tudor Princesses	4

Sunday Afternoons at the Parish Church of a Scottish University City	6 6
TAYLOR's (Jeremy) Works, edited by EDEN	15
———— (E.) Selections from some Contemporary Poets	18
TENNENT's Ceylon	9
THIRLWALL's History of Greece	2
TIMBS's Curiosities of London	17
THOMSON's (Archbishop) Laws of Thought	5
———— (A. T.) Conspectus	10
Three Fountains (The)	19
TODD (A.) on Parliamentary Government	1
———— and BOWMAN's Anatomy and Physiology of Man	10
TRENCH's Realities of Irish Life	2
TROLLOPE's Barchester Towers	17
———— Warden	17
TWISS's Law of Nations	20
TYNDALL's Lectures on Heat	8
———— Lectures on Sound	8
———— Memoir of FARADAY	4
Uncle PETER's Fairy Tale	17
URE's Dictionary of Arts, Manufactures, and Mines	12
VAN DER HOEVEN's Handbook of Zoology	8
VENTOUILLAC's French Poetry	18
WARBURTON's Hunting Songs	19
WATSON's Principles and Practice of Physic	10
WATTS's Dictionary of Chemistry	9
WEBB's Objects for Common Telescopes	7
WEBSTER & WILKINSON's Greek Testament	14
WELLINGTON's Life, by GLEIG	3
WELLS on Dew	8
WEST on Children's Diseases	10
———— on Nursing Children	20
WHATELY's English Synonymes	5
———— Life and Correspondence	3
———— Logic	5
———— Rhetoric	5
———— on Religious Worship	16
Whist, what to Lead, by CAM	20
WHITE and RIDDLE's Latin-English Dictionaries	5
WILCOCKS's Sea Fisherman	19
WILLICH's Popular Tables	20
WINSLOW on Light	8
WOOD's (J. G.) Bible Animals	8
———— Homes without Hands	8
———— (T.) Chemical Notes	10
WOODWARD's Historical and Chronological Encyclopædia	3
WRIGHT's Homer's Iliad	18
YEO's Manual of Zoology	8
YONGE's English-Greek Lexicons	5
———— Two Editions of Horace	18
YOUATT on the Dog	19
———— on the Horse	19
ZELLER's Socrates	3

www.ingramcontent.com/pod-product-compliance
Lightning Source LLC
Chambersburg PA
CBHW022133160426
43197CB00009B/1266